Heloise

GET ORGANIZED WITH

Also by Heloise:

HELOISE CONQUERS STINKS AND STAINS

IN THE KITCHEN WITH HELOISE

HELOISE FROM A TO Z

ALL NEW HINTS FROM HELOISE

Heloise®

GET ORGANIZED WITH
Heloise

A Perigee Book

P

A Perigee Book
Published by The Berkley Publishing Group
A division of Penguin Group (USA) Inc.
375 Hudson Street
New York, New York 10014

Copyright © 2004 by Heloise, Inc.
Cover design by Dorothy Wachtenheim
Cover photo by Michael Keel copyright © King Features Syndicate, Inc., and Penguin Group (USA) Inc.
Text design by Tiffany Estreicher

Perigee trade paperback edition: January 2004

Visit out website at www.penguin.com

Library of Congress Cataloging-in-Publication Data

Get organized with Heloise.
p. cm.
ISBN 0-399-52941-1
1. Home economics. 2. Time management.   I. Heloise.

TX147.G44 2004
640—dc22

2003065638

Printed in the United States of America

10 9 8 7 6 5 4 3 2

Acknowledgments

So many people to thank! Merry Clark, editorial director of Heloise, Inc., as always makes my job look easy! John Duff, publisher, Perigee Books, my other favorite team member who nudges just a little when I need it. My Heloise Central gang in San Antonio, Texas: Ruth, Jane, Kelly, Joyce, and Brucette who are all fabulous to work with. I don't know what I would do without them! All of the wonderful Heloise readers who shared their organizing hints. My mother, the original Heloise, who taught me how to pack a suitcase and organize a pantry so I can tell at a quick glance what I need to buy. My dear lovable husband, David who really knows how to organize everything from his fishing gear to hot air balloon equipment! Many thanks to all who helped.

CONTENTS

Introduction ix

1. Organizing Basics 1

PART ONE
Organized Around the House

2. The Kitchen 13
3. The Living Room, Bedrooms, and Closets 29
4. Bathrooms and the Laundry Room 50
5. The Garage, Attic, and Basement 62

PART TWO
Keeping Your Family Organized

6. Kids' Stuff 73
7. Pets 82
8. Personal Organizing 91
9. Entertaining 107

PART THREE

Organized and on the Go

10. Shopping   125

11. Travel and Vacations   139

12. Moving   157

    Index   171

Introduction

The very thought of getting organized, for many of us, seems overwhelming. With our too-busy daily lives, there never seems to be enough time to get our homes into a clutter-free, chaos-controlled state. But organizing doesn't have to be a drag! As I've learned over the years, it *is* possible to get a handle on it!

For some of us, it's easier than for others. I was lucky enough to grow up in a military household with my daddy, Air Force colonel Mike Cruse (Ret.), and with a mother named Heloise. We moved a lot, and they taught me at an early age how to "sort out and throw out"—a lesson that has served me well over the years.

My mother, the original Heloise, was a great believer in doing things "when you are in the mood." She said that "rearranging" was a way to be good to yourself, because it gives you extra time in your day to engage in other, more enjoyable, pursuits. She also wrote, "Time is the greatest gift from God. What we save, we can utilize elsewhere. You need time to enjoy yourself. Think how many times a day you go to your cabinets to find something. If you could find what you are looking for each time in one less second, and add those seconds up . . . see what you have saved."

There's no better reason to get organized. So here are some *aha!* hints to make this job easier for you. Fortunately, not only did I have my parents' wisdom, but readers of my internationally syndicated newspaper and *Good Housekeeping* magazine columns have shared their tried-and-true organizing and clutter-controlling hints. I have been writing about and answering questions on this topic for years. So I've brought together my favorite Reader Hints, along with the Organizing Hints I've shared, plus Classic Hints from my mother and Budget Organizing tips. Remember, there's no right or wrong way or set-in-stone rules for organizing, but rather what works best for you.

1

Organizing Basics

Keeping a home organized is an ongoing process: As soon as everything is picked up and put away, those little clutter gremlins inevitably strike again. And the only way to keep your sanity is to keep your sense of humor when it comes to the clutter wars.

You know it's time to take action if you are constantly losing things right in your own home. When you just can't find what you're looking for after an intense search, you've probably accumulated too much space-hogging, closet-cramming stuff! The good news is, an organizing crisis can be just the thing to make you focus on better habits.

Three Keys to Getting Started

The More Often You Use Something, the Closer It Needs to Be

As you enter a room, take a long, hard look, assessing all the objects according to use: Are the things you use the most close at hand? Are the items least-used stored farther away? Are the items that have not been touched in a year still there, or should they be in the attic or garage—or tossed?

Use It or Lose It

When you are in a good mood to organize (or in a bad mood that makes you want to throw things out), start tossing the useless, broken, or yucky stuff into the trash, and give things in good condition away to charity. (If family members hate to part with items, give each of them two boxes and let them keep things inside that will be held for six months. If they don't use those items within that time, out they go!)

The Right Stuff in the Right Place

Next, take a look at everything you've kept. Are your useful things not where they belong? Are your children's clothes in a pile on the floor or their toys strewn everywhere? Make certain you have the right size drawers, closets, and bins to hold things in an organized fashion. Show your family that there's a proper place for everything.

With this approach, organizing becomes more logical. Once you decide where things belong, try to keep them to their designated spots by returning them immediately after each use. Just establishing order will make finding things when you need them much easier—and help make your home life less stressful.

The "5-Minutes or 5-Things" Daily Plan

To prevent chaos from taking over, I try to tackle clutter with my 5-Minutes or 5-Things Daily Plan. Set aside five minutes—minimum—every day, and simply use it to focus on one organizing task. You'll be surprised at how much you can accomplish in this amount of time. Or use your spare time to cull five things: Pick up, put away, pass on, or throw out five items from a drawer, shelf, closet, etc.

For example, you might:

- Put away countertop clutter.

- Take out the garbage.

- Bundle newspapers and magazines.

- Sort a drawer of knickknacks.

- Rearrange a bookshelf.

I often put this plan to use when I am watching television. During the commercials, I get up and pick up the living room. (The first time I did this, my husband thought I was crazy, jumping up and down!) My editorial director, Merry, adopted this "TV-Commercial Cleaning Method" to give all the rugs in her home a fast once-over vacuum during the commercials in her favorite show. So don't waste time during commercial breaks—

ARE YOU A CLUTTER BUG?

I hate to throw away anything because . . .

> A.   It has sentimental value to me.
>
> B.   I might need it someday.
>
> C.   It's too overwhelming to think about.

My drawers are crammed because . . .

> A.   I don't have enough storage space.
>
> B.   I don't mind taking time to search for what I need.
>
> C.   My husband promised to clean them out, but he hasn't yet.

I don't organize because . . .

> A.   It won't make that much of a difference, will it?
>
> B.   Everything will just get messy again.
>
> C.   I don't have the time.

If you agree with any of these statements, you are a clutter bug! But read on. You absolutely can get organized. And organizing your time and possessions can make a positive change in your life.

by the end of the program, you can have a clean and organized room.

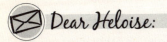 *Dear Heloise:*

As a full-time professional woman with a large home to care for, I found myself dreading weekends because of the tasks ahead of me. Then I hit on the idea of using my stereo to help me get through tedious jobs. I estimate the time it will take, then put on one, two, or more CDs. If the music is still playing when the job is finished, I have won the game. This makes chores more enjoyable because the rhythm gets me cleaning with a beat.

Dear Reader: **A great idea for making organizing more pleasant—it sounds like music to my ears!**

Make Organizing Easy as A-B-C

Here's an easy way to take stock of what you have and get rid of clutter. With this method, establishing order in any cabinet, drawer, shelf, or closet can be as simple as A-B-C.

1. Remove everything from the area and sort items into three piles:

   A. Items used almost every day.
   B. Items brought out only for seasonal or special occasions.
   C. Items that have not been used in more than a year or two, excluding those in group B.

2. Get rid of all items in group C. (If you can't bear to toss out anything right away, put the C items into a box, date and

label and put it away in the attic or garage. If you haven't touched them in a year, you most likely won't use them again. Throw them away, put them in your next garage sale, or donate them.)

3. Place B items in the back of the drawer or cabinet, or put them in a separate storage bin.

4. Place A items in the front, where they are easily accessible.

Organizing for the Good of It

A-B-C is one of my favorite organizing methods, but we all know that culling is sometimes easier said than done. Many of us are emotionally attached to items we have but don't need. I once kept a business suit that was way out of fashion—even though I hadn't worn it in ten years—because I signed my first book contract while wearing it.

I think it's easier to part with beloved clutter if you know you are giving it to another good home. Many worthy local and national organizations have wish lists for items they desperately need. Every room in your house has something that can be used by them or someone else. Call the group to see what they are looking for, then check your home and gather up all the things you no longer use. For example:

- Animal shelters and humane societies need old towels, sheets, or washers and dryers.

- Battered women's shelters and children's charities need clothing, luggage, soap, and personal items.

- Food banks and pantries can use food, canned goods, and other kitchen items.

- Libraries, prisons, nursing homes, and hospitals may be grateful for book and magazine donations.

- Schools or charity organizations may accept donations of computers and office equipment.

- Many charities will even take old cars—in fact, I donated my mother's 1977 Thunderbird to one such foundation.

You just may feel better knowing your stuff is moving to help others.

Give Yourself a Break— and Make a To-Do List

Many people don't like to sit down and write lists, but I've found that planning ahead, prioritizing, and taking a little time to organize really does save time, not to mention money, in the long run. When the day's activities are listed on one piece of paper, scheduling is easier. You might find you have time to go grocery shopping while the kids are at baseball practice. And no more coming home exhausted after running errands and realizing you forgot to pick up the dry cleaning!

Even the busiest person needs to sit down and rest once in a while, and if you're the kind of person who needs an excuse to take a break, use list-making time as your excuse. As you write, think about how organizing can help make you manage your home more effectively. We all feel better when we are running our homes and schedules instead of having our homes and schedules run us.

Heloise's Emergency Organizing Kit

Don't get caught without the right organizing tools! To help you de-clutter, always keep these essential items on hand:

- ☐ Binders, folders, and tabs
- ☐ Clothespins
- ☐ Glass or plastic jars of all sizes
- ☐ Glue sticks
- ☐ Permanent markers
- ☐ Push pins (tacks)
- ☐ Rubber bands
- ☐ Safety pins
- ☐ Scissors
- ☐ Sealable plastic bags
- ☐ Sewing kit
- ☐ Stapler and staples
- ☐ Stick-on labels
- ☐ String or twine
- ☐ Trash, paper, or paper bags
- ☐ White adhesive tape for labeling

Storage Aids Readily Available!

It's hard to stay neat if your possessions don't have a proper place in your home. Fortunately for organizationally challenged people, there are many commercial products available that can help you get organized, from installable closet and modular systems to ready-to-use storage containers for every room in the house.

Department, discount, hardware, and home improvement stores offer an incredible number of storage units that won't require a Ph.D. to set up. However, with a little ingenuity you can make your own budget storage systems; examples can be found in each chapter of this book. Look for baskets and containers of all kinds at garage sales. Transform routine household items into storage bins. For example, a large plastic garbage can is a great storage container for seasonal decorations. Fill it to the brim with items you want to hide away, and place the lid on upside down. Top it off with a round piece of plywood, and cover it with a floor-length tablecloth. You now have a lamp table and storage unit for any room in your house. (There are no excuses for not storing the things you want to keep in an attractive way.) And remember, every nook and cranny in your house can potentially be used for storage. Be imaginative and innovative.

Even if you *still* can't get organized, there are new devices for the hopelessly challenged—electronic locators! Attach these tags to an item, and if it goes missing, you can press a button and a base station will send an electronic signal to the lost item, which will beep until it's found. Unfortunately, I don't think there are enough tags to do the contents of a whole house! So it's worth it to get into the trenches and establish a place for everything in your home.

Heloise's Favorite Storage Aids

Baskets	Metal racks
Bookcases	Peg-Board
Cardboard boxes	Plastic hangers
Filing cabinets	Plastic see-through bins
Garbage cans	Shelves
Hampers	Wire baskets
Hooks	

Most of us have specific things that bother us when we're try-ing to keep the house clean and organized—mine is countertop clutter. So when you begin to organize, focus immediately on those one or two "problem areas" that are important to you. Take five minutes or cull five things. Make tossing clutter as easy as A-B-C. And when there seems to be too much to do at once, create a list to set priorities.

Taking one small organizing step is like putting your toes in the water. Pretty soon you'll be ready to jump into the pool!

PART ONE

Organized Around the House

2

The Kitchen

*"We spend most of our waking hours in
the kitchen. So keep it simple."* —the original Heloise

In most of our homes, the kitchen is the hub of daily activity. Keeping order here is a daily task. *Getting* your kitchen organized in the first place will make cooking and cleaning more efficient and less frustrating. But *keeping* your kitchen organized is not easy with so much going on and so many people coming and going.

To control chaos, you have to set guidelines for everyone who uses the kitchen. When my husband's son Russell came to live with us, I gave him a guided tour of the kitchen and the pantry so he knew where everything was. I told him that he had to clean up after he snacked or ate. That meant putting food back into the refrigerator or cabinet, rinsing and placing the dishes into the dishwasher, and wiping up any mess. Your children and everyone else in the house can learn to keep the kitchen organized by following your rules.

Every household has its own kitchen rules, but I think these two are essential:

1. *Clean as you go.* Wipe up stains and messes on the countertop and floor right away. Soak pots and pans that need it immediately after use. Put used plates and glasses into the dishwasher (if you have one), or wash them when you are finished eating. Keep an attractive container filled with water by the sink, and put all silverware inside it to soak— and not down the garbage disposal!

2. *Put away food.* Food not stored properly spoils faster and may attract pests.

5-Minutes or 5-Things

In five minutes, you can:

- Put away clean dishes
- Put dirty dishes into the dishwasher
- Set the table
- Organize a spice rack

Five things to throw away:

- Outdated cleaning products
- Expired items from the refrigerator
- Old, ratty sponges
- Dented cans
- Broken utensils

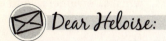 *Dear Heloise:*

I cook all the time and love my food highly seasoned. I organize my spices in alphabetical order in the cabinet above my counter working space so they're easy to find quickly when I need to add them to a dish.

General Kitchen Organizing Hints

- Keep cheap paper plates on hand; they are really handy. They can be used:

  - As a throwaway spoon rest
  - As a cutting board
  - As a dustpan
  - In the microwave, placed under cups as a spill-catcher or placed over the top of food to avoid a mess
  - For a quick meal—no dishes to wash!

- Store most frequently used pots, pans, utensils, dishes, and silverware in the most accessible places in cabinets and drawers.

- Store gadgets or appliances that you don't use regularly on a high shelf.

- Hang bulky items like graters and colanders on the inside of a pantry closet door.

- Place utensils used daily in a decorative jar on the counter for quick access.

■ Hang slotted spoons, skimmers, whisks, strainers, and other utensils too large or bulky for kitchen drawers on a Peg-Board, painted to match your kitchen.

■ Place a roll of plastic garbage bags in the bottom of your trash can. When you need a bag, you'll know exactly where it is.

■ Don't throw out those corks from wine and other bottles. Instead, wash them and use them to cover the tips of knives, barbecue forks, or kabob skewers. This will protect your fingers when you grab them out of the drawer.

■ Save glass jars that held olives, pickles, mayo, or jelly. Wash them well and use to hold items in your "junk" drawer like rubber bands or paper clips. These are great because you can see what's inside.

■ Put knives on a magnetized rack on the kitchen wall close to where you use them most often, to save drawer space.

Budget Organizing

Save those green plastic baskets that strawberries come in. They can be reused to:

▪ Hold soap and scouring pads around the sink.

▪ Store packets of sauce or soup mixes and spices in the cupboard.

▪ Contain holiday candy. Weave ribbons through the holes or attach appropriate decorations with glue.

Dear Heloise:

Do you hunt in vain for those elusive instruction booklets when an appliance breaks down? Well, we did, too, until we happened upon a simple solution. We now keep an envelope in the kitchen drawer to hold all the instruction booklets and guarantees for everything from the can opener to the lawn mower. This has prevented many frayed nerves and probably some service calls.

Drawers and Cabinets

Kitchen drawers and cabinets are places where stuff accumulates—from funnels to fondue pots. So use the A-B-C method and ask yourself these questions:

Do I:

- Really use every item in my kitchen?

- Absolutely need this item?

- Have to have all these pots and pans?

- Need three can openers?

- Use all these knives?

After you've finished sorting and discarding, measure the interior dimensions—width, depth, and height—of all your drawers and cabinets. Go to your favorite kitchenware or discount store to find organizing bins, racks, or dividers that fit the spaces and are appropriate for the types of items you will keep in them. For example:

- Use drawer dividers to separate large cooking utensils.

- A basket on a cabinet shelf is ideal for holding packaged foods such as cake mixes.

- Place frequently used cleansers in a plastic caddie for fast access.

- Attach metal racks on the ceiling or rods under your cabinets to hang frequently used pots and pans.

- Mount shelves on the inside of cabinet doors.

- Use two-tier turntables to organize spices and dried herbs.

- Store fruits and vegetables, measuring cups and spoons, or anything else in hanging three-tiered wire baskets.

- Put inexpensive push lights on the underside of shelves in dark cabinets to illuminate when needed.

Budget Organizing

Don't throw out margarine tubs or yogurt cups with lids. They can be used to hold all sorts of small items, such as corncob holders, toothpicks, twist-ties, magnets, paper clips, and push pins. Just write the contents on the lid with a marker, and you'll never have to waste time looking through your "junk" drawer for these little but invaluable things.

My mother loved to line cabinet shelves with aluminum foil because, as she said, "It reflects light. These cabinets are dark. It can be wiped with a sponge when it gets dirty and after using and reusing can be turned over the next time you clean the cabinet." She also suggested putting wax paper down first as a liner. I think it's a good idea to line shelves with shelf paper or wallpaper remnants. Some budget choices include plastic place mats, last year's laminated tablecloths, old posters, and gift wrap. You can cut these to fit.

But if you're going to be pulling lots of pots and pans out of a cabinet, you may want to consider laying vinyl floor tiles, which are easy to install. Just cut to fit and peel off the backing. These are more expensive than shelf liners, but they will hold up better and be easy to maintain simply by wiping them clean.

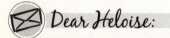 *Dear Heloise:*

Immediately after cleaning out and reorganizing a cabinet, I take a snapshot. Then I laminate each photo (you can buy laminating film at a discount or office-supply store) and tape it inside the door. Now, anyone who is responsible for putting things away in the kitchen can see where the items are supposed to go. My husband thinks it is a great idea!

Dear Reader: I do, too, and it can work for any type of storage space.

Dear Heloise:

I nailed my breadbox to the underside of my kitchen cabinets to create extra counter space.

Dear Reader: This is a great idea, but be careful not to cover up the vent holes. If the air can't circulate, bread will get moldy faster. You also can buy small appliances such as can openers, coffeemakers, and toaster ovens that can be mounted under the cabinet.

Cabinets Under the Sink

You can use the A-B-C organizing system for under-the-sink storage, too. For most of us, keeping track and keeping order of all the cleaners we use can be tough to do regularly. Get all the products out and ask yourself these questions:

- Do I really use all of them?

- Are they too old?

- Has the liquid evaporated or is the container leaking?

- Could any of these products be dangerous to my curious children or pets if they get into the cabinets?

- Where else could I store them more safely?

Then reorganize all of the products by use. Put those you utilize most often up front, and place those less frequently needed in the back. Store them in plastic buckets or pails, so if they leak or spill, they won't damage the inside of the cabinet. (Be sure to wash the inside of the cabinet with a disinfectant, then let the area dry thoroughly before returning the cleaning products.)

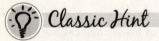 Classic Hint

When organizing the area under your kitchen sink, start by putting a few layers of newspaper on the floor and then place everything from the cabinet on the paper. The newspapers will prevent spots and rings on your floor. When you get through organizing, you can just roll up the newspapers, throw them out, and save more cleaning up.

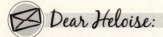 *Dear Heloise:*

I put all frequently used household cleaners, cloths, and sponges in a box that I can carry around. No more going back and forth to the cabinet to get another cleaner. I do the same in each bathroom and the garage.

Dear Reader: Saves you time, and best of all, this way everyone in the household knows where the cleaning supplies are.

The Pantry

I have always had a well-stocked pantry to keep everything we need on hand so we don't run out of supplies. My husband loves to rummage through the inventory and choose what he wants to eat. But how do I keep it organized? With a system of color-coded food shelves originally created by my colorful mother (see the accompanying box). I have used this color system all my life, and not only does it make organizing quicker, it's also great for children, too.

I also write the expiration date on the top of each can or box with a felt-tip pen and place items by shelf from front to back according to the date. Date and put new canned goods at the *back* of shelves.

According to the Canned Food Information Council, most canned foods remain good for two years, if they are stored properly. Cans should be stored in a dry place with moderately cool temperatures, never freezing or in extreme heat. Never put canned goods near furnaces, radiators, steam pipes, or kitchen ranges. Dampness can cause cans to rust.

 *Classic Hint*

Here's a simple way to arrange shelves—food storage by color:

Green shelf: canned peas, pickles, green beans, asparagus, spinach
Red shelf: canned beets, tomatoes, tomato sauce, cranberries, pimentos, cherries
Orange shelf: canned yams, carrots, peaches
Yellow shelf: canned corn, pineapple, mayonnaise
White shelf: macaroni, applesauce, sauerkraut, onions, pears, potatoes

In another cabinet or shelf, put all your condiments and spreads. Use another shelf for dried and boxed goods, such as biscuit mix, rice, and so forth. Then pick the most convenient shelf possible and put all your breakfast cereals here. Make it easy for the kids to help themselves!

Now, you don't have to use an entire shelf for each color. If you have only three shelves in your home for canned goods, divide those in halves or thirds and do the best you can.

Then when you go to the store, it's no trouble to make a list or recall, "I am low on green things."

■ Put grains, flour, and other staples into tightly sealed glass canisters. You can see what you need at a glance, and this also will prevent insects from invading these foods.

■ Organize your pantry by categories. Store paper towels, plastic baggies, aluminum foil, etc. in one area. Place canned goods with the expiration dates in front or on a specific shelf so they can be used before they spoil.

- Separate the food you use on a daily basis—teas, coffee, sugar, and spices. Make them readily accessible. Foods you use only occasionally can be put higher up or at the back of the shelves.

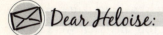 ## Dear Heloise:

For a number of years, I have used my pantry to store all of my everyday dishes and glassware, using the floor for large items, steamers, pressure cookers, etc. The extensive use of cup hooks neatens the pantry and ensures that I do not have to hunt through the food cabinets for a special cup or glass.

Dear Reader: Hooks are great for organizing because they free up more shelf space for storage. You can also put plastic bins under the bottom shelf in your pantry to hold pet food, paper towels, and other kitchen supplies. And did you know that rectangular dishpans can double your self-storage capacity when you fill and stack them?

Budget Organizing

Don't throw out the paper towel cardboard cores.

- Use them to hold extension or appliance cords in the kitchen.

- Flatten the cores and put knives inside to protect your fingers from the points.

- Wrap ribbon around cores so it stays untangled.

- Make a boot tree by taping several together.

Refrigerator and Freezer

While most refrigerators have pre-set spaces for some items, such as a dairy section, crisper, or meat keeper, I organize my refrigerator by designating parking spaces for specific foods on the top, middle, bottom, and door shelves. I put dairy products like butter, yogurt, and cheese on the top shelf; leftovers on the second shelf; and so on. I keep leftovers in glass jars at the front of the shelf so they can be used up quickly. With an organized refrigerator, everyone knows where to find the foods they want.

- Keep the most frequently consumed foods in front.

- Designate one shelf or area for all leftovers. Use see-through containers to quickly identify what's inside.

- Tape or use a magnet to hold a list of leftovers to the refrigerator door.

- Check the refrigerator often, and toss out dated or old foodstuffs. Before a weekly shopping trip is a good time to do this, as you can take inventory and make your shopping list at the same time.

Dear Heloise:

I divide up foods bought in bulk by using an airtight sealing appliance that helps increase some foods' shelf life. This came in real handy when I found that my power had been off for seven days while I was away! Everything in my freezer except ice was in these sealed bags. So cleanup was unbelievably easy.

Dear Reader: Protecting foods in the freezer by sealing is a good habit for daily use—and if a disaster strikes!

My most important freezer hint: Don't let it become a warehouse for antique food! Even if you are in a hurry to get food into the freezer, don't toss or stuff it inside because it will be harder to find when you want it.

- Label the contents and date all frozen food items with masking tape and a marker. You can also write on some frozen food packages.

- Put the most frequently used foods in the front or in the door so they can be found quickly and the freezer will stay cool.

- Put items into the freezer in a way that they do not block the cold airflow. Look inside your freezer to determine where the flow comes from, possibly the top rear of the freezer. Or check the owner's manual.

- Freeze stews and soups or other leftovers in sealable plastic bags. They can lie flat on top of each other and save space. Depending on the size and shape of your freezer, you also can save space by freezing soups and casseroles in square or loaf pans. They are easier to stack.

- Freeze leftovers in the shape of the pot or pan you plan to reheat them in. Line the pot with foil or plastic wrap and then put in the leftovers. Cover the food with the remaining wrap, and put it into the freezer. When the leftovers are frozen, take the food out.

■ Utilize wire or plastic mesh baskets to hold categories of food in the freezer. Then you can just lift out one basket to get at the items.

■ Don't freeze too many items at one time. The heat emitted by warm foods can raise the temperature of the freezer. Let warm items cool in the refrigerator before freezing, or place warm packages away from frozen ones. Some upright freezers have a separate quick-freeze shelf.

■ Cut labels from food packages and tape them to the storage container to easily identify what's inside.

■ Tape or use a magnet to hold an inventory sheet to the freezer door. Record the dates the items were put into the freezer. Check them off the list when you use them. That way, you'll know what to replace.

■ Label everything. Once frozen, many foods look the same even if you've put them in see-through containers. You may just grab the wrong thing!

If you know you don't clean out your fridge and freezer often enough, you're not alone. I asked my readers to write to me about what was the oldest or most bizarre food item in their refrigerator. Some of the responses included a 55-year-old jar of pear preserves, a 37-year-old jar of pickled pig's feet, and a 53-year-old Christmas fruitcake. Many had saved champagne and pieces of cake from their weddings, and others kept food from memorable trips or honeymoons.

If you can't bear to throw away these aged keepsakes, be sure to label them clearly—otherwise a family member or guest might accidentally eat them.

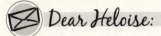 *Dear Heloise:*

I make a spreadsheet of the contents and date of items in my freezer. I then print the chart, insert it into a plastic sheet protector, and place it on the side of my refrigerator with decorative magnets. As I use something, I strike through it on the list with a black erasable pen. This is especially helpful for knowing what is in the freezer, what needs to be used, and what needs to be placed on the shopping list.

Dear Heloise:

Here is a quick and easy way to use the items in your freezer in the appropriate order. Put a colored dot on them to correspond to the month before which they should be used. Each month in the year should be designated by a different color: red for January, yellow for February, etc. That way, there is no doubt that a package of hamburger frozen in January gets used before one from February, and so on. I keep a master list of color codes on the freezer door. It not only keeps your freezer in order, but small children love to help put the dots on and retrieve items for you to show you that they know their colors.

Organizing Your Kitchen for Safety

The kitchen can be a dangerous place, so be careful in how you organize kitchenware and products. If you have small children, take a close look at what potentially could hurt them and reorganize so these items are out of harm's way.

- Baby-proof your kitchen with special latches for drawers and cabinets.

- Store knives and other sharp items up and out of children's reach.

- Turn pot handles away from the front of the stove when you are cooking to keep them out of a child's grasp.

- Keep household cleaners far from kids' inquiring reach. If you store them under the sink, be sure to keep a safety latch on the door.

- Keep appliance cords wrapped up and secured with a twist-tie, except for the length you need to plug it in. Long, hanging cords can be pulled by a child, sending an appliance toppling onto them.

In addition, be sure to have a list of important safety numbers, including the police department, fire department, poison control center, and family doctor, on the fridge or by the telephone.

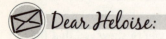 **Dear Heloise:**

Need to pull out a drawer just to find a spatula, spaghetti fork, or soup ladle because they all have the same shape and color handles? Turn the divider bin around so the handles point back, and you can immediately see what you are looking for.

Dear Reader: For table flatware and plastic this is a good idea, but for sharp items like knives, ice picks, or kabob skewers, it's better to store them with the handles to the front of the drawer. Always place these items in carefully to avoid a potential safety hazard.

3

The Living Room, Bedrooms, and Closets

After the kitchen, the living room and bedrooms are the most popular and most-used places in the house for people to spend time, so keeping them organized is a must.

These are the two general rules I've established in my family for these areas:

1. *What comes in goes out.* If you carry an item into a room from another area, you must also carry it out!

2. *Right stuff in the right place.* If you take out magazines, books, games, or anything else from where they are stored, they have to be returned after use!

Living Room

Before you tackle this room, remember to look at your space objectively. Ask yourself, are things here as organized and accessible as they could be? Does the room have enough bookshelves, cabinets, bins, or wicker baskets to hold all your things? If you find that clutter is constantly spilling out no matter how hard you try to keep the living room organized, you may need to rethink your storage tactics. Here are some ideas:

- Use large baskets or footlockers in the hidden spaces under tables with skirts and behind couches.

- Take advantage of the space under a window seat—or create a window seat with storage space.

- Utilize the tops of cabinets, bookshelves, breakfronts, china cabinets, and armoires for extra storage. Baskets and decorative boxes make ideal storage for these out-of-the-way but visible places.

- Keep mantels and tabletops as clutter-free as possible. This has a two-fold benefit: It's easier to dust and the room looks more organized.

- A large, attractive trunk used as a coffee table can double as a storage piece.

- Have one bin or basket for newspapers and one for magazines. Toss out on a regular basis, particularly in time for garbage or recycling collection.

5-Minutes or 5-Things

In five minutes, you can:

- Bundle old newspapers
- Put a roll of photos in an album

- Straighten and organize a bookshelf
- De-clutter the coffee table
- Organize videotapes, CDs, DVDs

Five things to put away:

- Books
- Toys
- Shoes
- Puzzles and games
- Remote controls

Budget Organizing

Maintain a decorating household information notebook. In it, record all floor and window dimensions to make buying new curtains or flooring much easier. List the different paint colors and brands. Glue paint chips, wallpaper and fabric swatches on the same page with the descriptions of each room. These are very helpful when buying accessories or rugs!

Create a Focal Point

Almost every room in my home is filled with photos. They make decorating personal and meaningful. My husband and I love hot-air ballooning, so we have many pictures and balloon replicas in our family room. Consider the "photographic heirlooms" you have—organize and display them!

I like to give the living room a focal point to make it instantly look more organized. Group pictures, favorite souvenirs, or personal collections into one area or on one shelf. They will be a more attractive display all together than scattered around your home. Photos can be framed in similar style—wood or metal. In addition, you can cluster things together that are made from the same material, such as wood, porcelain, shell or brass. Don't worry about different shapes or sizes; they will all match.

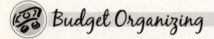 ## Budget Organizing

Paint old ladders to use for storage in different rooms. You can store books, plants, or just about anything on them. I have a friend who puts her cowboy boots on a colorful ladder in her bedroom and heard from a reader who hangs bright afghans on an old ladder for display. The ladder can be hung on the wall, leaned against the wall or stand open in a corner.

Wall Hangings

You can hang just about anything on your walls. I have a friend who loves hats. She has her bedroom walls covered with colorful hats and a second bedroom wall decorated with her wild collection of sunglasses. Another woman loves animals and has a menagerie of exquisite animal paintings on her living room walls.

- Frame needlepoint projects. Hang quilts from a wooden rod by attaching wooden rings to them.

■ Frame something that has a special meaning to you—from children's artwork to family documents.

■ Arrange your family's life story in photos—from weddings to grandchildren—on the wall in a long hallway. Try to keep the frames of a similar style, color, or material for a neater look.

How to Hang Pictures

■ Don't just eyeball the right place on the wall to hang a picture. Before you put the nail or picture hanger in the wall, measure with tape and a yardstick.

■ Before hanging an arrangement of pictures, make an outline of each of the frames from newspaper or wrapping paper. Tape each outline to the wall (or use straight pins) to see how the arrangement will fit. Then you can place the nail hooks through the paper into the wall. Tear off the paper and hang the pictures.

■ When hanging pictures from molding, use transparent nylon instead of picture wire. It's almost invisible.

■ If hanging pictures on a plaster wall, form an X over the nails with two strips of transparent or masking tape to prevent crumbling.

■ When you repaint a room, preserve the grouping by inserting toothpicks into the hook holes and painting over them. Then after the paint dries, remove the toothpicks and rehang the pictures.

Organizing Photos

I think all of us have boxes or piles of photos that we just don't have time to put into albums. But it's important to do that to save these memories—photos not stored properly, can become curled, creased, or cracked. Use my A-B-C method to quickly sort out and save the best ones; toss the others (If you have a digital camera, simply print the good ones!)

■ Be sure to identify everyone in the photo, write the date (some cameras automatically date) and place on the back. Years later, you'll be glad you did.

■ Fires, floods, and other disasters happen everywhere and all of your photos can be lost. To preserve valuable family photos, either get an extra set made or scan them in your computer. Keep the extras in a safe place.

■ If photos are really old, it may be best to take them to a frame shop or professional photography studio to have them preserved or reprinted.

■ If new photos have become curled, put them between the pages of a big, heavy book to uncurl. Or, with your iron on cool, place photos picture-side down and very carefully iron them flat. Be sure not to have the iron on the steam setting.

■ Frame photos or store them in albums. Use a non-polyvinyl chloride plastic that does not have any adhesive on the pages, so the pictures don't stick to them. Glue can permanently adhere photos to the pages, and you may not be able to remove them later without damage.

✉ *Dear Heloise:*

Before I send out school pictures or Christmas photos of the family or the kids, I always create labels for each one detailing names, ages, and dates and stick it to the back of the photo. I'll even type in a funny saying if the picture warrants one.

✉ *Dear Heloise:*

When my husband visits his mother, who has dementia, he takes old and recent family photos with him to help conversation. She is delighted to see and be reminded of past relatives and friends as well as seeing pictures of her children, grandchildren, and great-grandchildren. Needless to say, they now have much more to talk about.

Dear Reader: What a picture-perfect way to remind those who may have some memory loss. A photo can put a face to a forgotten name and it's a wonderful way to start a conversation.

Books

I once was in a bookstore for a signing and a store employee pointed out the section stocked with books on organizing, noting what a mess it was! Organizing a bookshelf takes time and patience, but here are a few invaluable hints:

- Color-code books with colored peel-off dots by category—fiction, nonfiction, biography, self-help, mysteries, romances, history, gardening, hobbies, etc. This way you can display books neatly on a shelf by size and still identify the categories quickly.

■ Sort through all of your family's books several times a year. Give old paperbacks to hospitals, schools, nursing homes, libraries, or charities.

■ Dust and clean books at least once a month. For old or valuable books, this is important so they don't deteriorate.

■ To prevent musty odors, store books in a dry place. Put activated charcoal in an old sock in the box along with the books. And never store books in a damp basement!

■ Any shelf can do double-duty by placing a ledge—made from a cut-to-length two-by-four—at the back. Small paperbacks can fit on the ledge and a row of books can be placed in front.

■ A stack of attractive oversized books can be placed under a coffee or end table.

 Budget Organizing

Reuse those large popcorn tins around the house to:

• Store skeins of yarn, needlepoint, or other sewing projects

• Hoid magazines upright

• Keep small children's toys and games out of sight

Home Electronics

■ Keep television, VCR, DVD, or CD player remote controls and gadgets in a basket or bowl near the machines.

- Color-code records, CDs, videotapes, and DVDs with colored stick-on dots according to categories, then you won't have to go through them all to find the one you want. Records, CDs, and cassettes can be categorized by pop, rock, jazz, country, classical, and western, etc. Videotapes and DVDs can be arranged by comedy, drama, family films. Label them clearly and keep upright on shelves.

- Do not stack videotapes, DVDs, or anything else on top of the recorder.

- Store videotapes vertically. Fast-forward and rewind tapes at least once a year.

- Store videotapes away from the heat and don't take them from cool to warm places right before playing them.

- To identify shows you've taped, save the reviews and tape onto the jacket or the cassette.

Dear Heloise:

We spend many hours watching videotapes of shows we've recorded. We've acquired quite a collection, and in order to quickly find a particular episode we'd like to watch, we have a loose-leaf binder with all our tapes numbered and a brief description of the episodes. We can quickly scan the list and find out which tape we want.

Bedrooms

Bedrooms have now become multi-activity rooms for reading, exercising, eating, watching television, and dressing—not to mention sleeping! But this is the one room in which you should feel most relaxed, so to keep the chaos at bay, straighten up as you go. Aside from making you feel anxious, piles of clothes, books, magazines, and exercise equipment left on the floor can be dangerous and cause accidents.

5-Minutes or 5-Things

In five minutes, you can:

- Make your bed
- Organize a shoe rack
- Pick out your clothes for the next day
- Sort and recycle unused wire hangers
- Straighten your dresser top or nightstand

Five things to put away:

- Shoes
- Dirty clothes
- Makeup
- Reading material
- Exercise gear

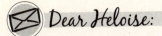 Dear Heloise:

I used to have an exercise bike in my bedroom, until I got up in the middle of the night and tripped over it in the dark. I spent a year recovering from my injuries!

Dear Reader: Paths from the bed to the bathroom and the hallways in your home should always be clear. Put away exercise equipment or anything else you can trip over right after using. Do a quick check before going to sleep, use night-lights where you can, and always keep a flashlight handy.

■ Use the space under your bed for storage. You can easily find flat or rolling cardboard or plastic containers that slide under the bed. Storing out-of-season clothes or linens for the bedroom in these boxes will create more room in the closet.

■ Divide and conquer for drawer organizing. Separate all items by category.

■ Utilize the back of closet doors for more storage, especially out-of-season items. Hanging hooks are available at hardware and department stores.

■ Designate a bowl, dish, platter, or basket to hold everything that comes out of your pockets when you take off your clothes. Then you will know where your wallet, change, and keys are.

■ Have one place for jewelry. Get a basket, felt-lined jewelry box, or holder to put your rings, watch, necklaces, and earrings in when you take them off at night.

■ For an easy place to hang necklaces and bracelets, you can hammer nails, attach suction cups, or stick rods inside your closet or on a bulletin board.

- Install large hooks on the walls of your closet to hang purses, belts, or scarves.

- Organize shoes on floor racks, in hanging arrangers, or on the inside of your closet door. Or keep shoes in boxes. Label each one so you know what's inside. They can be stacked on a floor, on open shelves, or on the top shelf of the closet—and still look neat!

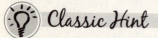 Budget Organizing

To arrange small items in drawers, recycle containers from other parts of your home. For example, muffin tins, foam egg cartons, or ice cube trays can be put into drawers to hold earrings, buttons, bobby pins, or cuff links. Old shoe boxes are perfect to keep socks and underwear from becoming a jumbled mess.

Classic Hint

Instead of hanging your hubby's pajamas in the closet, try placing them under his pillow. Do the same for your nightgown. This eliminates about fourteen footsteps a day—seven to the closet and seven back! Multiply that by 365 days a year, and see how many steps you will save! This is convenient in more ways than one. Your husband can't say, "I can't find my pajamas," and you haven't wasted 5,000 steps a year.

How to Organize Your Closet

1. Declutter

Cull all your clothes using the A-B-C method of organizing. Take all your clothes out of your closet and examine every item you have. Make three piles of clothing:

A. Clothing you wear frequently.
B. Clothing you seldom wear, or wear only for special occasions or seasonally.
C. Clothing that has not been worn for a year or more, or garments that are stained or damaged beyond repair. These do not go back into the closet.

Check to see if any of the clothes in the A pile need buttons or any repairs. After you return the A pile to the closet, review the B pile more closely. Remember, *use it or lose it!* Special occasion or out-of-season clothes can be stored elsewhere if you have the space or at the back of your closet. Other seldom-worn clothes may be reassigned to group C for discard or donation. All items in the C pile should now be sorted for discard or, if they are in good condition, for donation.

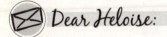 Dear Heloise:

I organize dark clothes in my closet using different colored clothes hangers. It's hard to tell black and blue items apart, but by putting them on the matching color hangers makes identification easy.

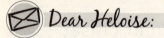 *Dear Heloise:*

I use plastic hangers in assorted colors by coding them: blue for blouses, red for slacks, yellow for skirts, white for dresses, and so on.

2. Rearrange

Does it seem like you never have closet space in your home? Is every single closet packed to the gills? Once you've decluttered, here are steps you can take to rearrange your closets better:

- Hang short items, such as skirts or shirts, vertically: Purchase eighteen inches of quarter-inch brass chain. Loop the chain over the closet rod, and secure it with a piece of wire by joining two links, and let the rest of the chain hang down. Place hangers through the links.

- Put hooks or over-the-closet hangers on the door to hold purses.

- Hang matching slacks and jackets or shirts on one sturdy hanger.

- Plastic milk crates can be stacked on their sides to hold sweaters, shoes, or handbags and then stacked on top of each other. Or put them on top of shelves for added space.

- Place old bookcases into closets. You have ready-made shelving for sweaters, shoes, or bags.

- Store seldom-used items in suitcases.

- Take advantage of space in the top of closets by installing more shelves or hanging racks.

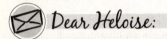

Dear Heloise:

I have a lot of shoes and always end up opening every shoe box to find a certain pair. So I bought clear shoe boxes, took instant pictures of all my shoes, taped the photos to the end of each box, and stacked the boxes on my closet shelf. My husband thought I was crazy when he saw me taking photos of my shoes—until he saw how organized and efficient it was! If I need a certain pair, I just look for their picture!

Dear Heloise:

When I buy shoes I keep them in the original box and then organize by season and color on the top shelf of my closet, with the description facing the front where I can read it. When shoes are not on my feet, they are off the floor and dust free.

3. Store

- Never return dirty clothes to the closet or trunk. Clean first, then store.

- Do not store leather or furs in plastic bags; they need air circulation. Cover them with old sheets or special commercial bags.

- Store clothing away from direct sunlight or strong artificial light. Some fabrics, especially silk, can fade.

- Clean heirloom clothing, like a wedding gown, and wrap first in unbleached muslin or acid-free white tissue paper. Store in a sealed box in a cool, dry spot.

Budget Organizing

Use plastic garbage cans with secure lids for storing seasonal clothing. Buy several when they are on sale. To fill for maximum space, lay the can on its side. First, pack the skirts; rolling them vertically from the hem to the waistband into a long, thin roll. Put the hem against the bottom of the can.

Then fold blazers, lining side out, tucking the shoulders into each other, and roll. Continue with slacks, vests, and dresses, which you roll from waist. By placing all the hem ends down, you have more room at the wider, top part of the can.

When the can is full, stand it up. Make an inventory of everything inside and put it on the top or attach a copy to the outside. Drop several cedar balls on top and then seal. Label the outside, and put it in the back of your closet, attic, or dry basement.

Planning Your Workweek Wardrobe

Take a few minutes during the weekend to plan your wardrobe for the week ahead. Make sure all your clothes are cleaned and in good repair, and hang everything in matching sets in the closet. If you can't decide on outfits that far in advance, at least pick out what you're going to wear the night before. Then you won't have to make decisions early in the morning. It will save you time!

If you change purses often, keep a box or basket handy just for the contents of your purse. When you come home, dump everything into the designated container. In the morning, if you decide to use a different purse from the day before, you'll know where everything is. To make it even easier, gather loose items such as pens, checkbook, cosmetics, and medications into plastic bags. Just grab the bags and put them into whatever handbag you are using that day. For more on organizing your purse, see page 133.

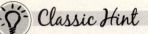

Classic Hint

Never clean a closet when you are not in a throwing-away mood. Wait until you are angry or really fed up with the mess! This is the best time to organize.

Say to yourself, "I have kept this dress for two years thinking I would wear it, but why not get rid of it?" Reducing the amount of things you have will automatically make it easier to keep your closets organized.

Discard the stuff. Give it away. Sell it!

Now, starting fresh, line the shelves and replace only the articles you have worn in the last year. Remember, be ruthless! If you haven't used it in a year or two, you probably never will.

Linen Closets

Proper storing and organizing of linens will make them easier to get to, keep them in better shape, and help them survive extensive family use longer. Once you find a system that works for you, it really is easier to organize the space you have. Here are a few of my hints:

- Organize bed linens into sets. Fold one flat sheet in the middle, fold it in half and then in half again (both folds the long way). Then fold a fitted sheet the same way, and lay it on top of the folded flat sheet. Add one or two pillowcases, each folded in half the long way also. Then roll them all together into one neat roll. The rolls stack better on your cupboard shelves, and family members can grab a roll instead of messing up all the linens. If you have different

45

sizes of beds, store bedding accordingly. (You can use the same roll-up technique for towel sets to keep bath towels, hand towels, and washcloths together.)

■ Fold tablecloths to avoid creases. Make the first fold down the middle with the right side out. Fold each side back toward and slightly beyond the center. If you do this, when the tablecloth is opened, the side crease will be the same and there won't be a dust streak down the center.

■ Install an adjustable tension curtain rod in the back of a small closet. If you are short on space, place table linens on hangers and cover with dry-cleaning or garbage bags.

■ Store extra bedding in an unused laundry hamper.

■ Place extra pillows in shams or decorative zipper cases. Pile them on beds or sofas.

■ Put sheets on unused beds; they won't take up room in the closet!

■ Roll or fold extra blankets to use in large pillow shams. I save the plastic zippered bags curtains, blankets, and comforters come in to use for storing pillows and blankets under the bed or on closet shelves. This helps keep them clean, too.

■ Keep extra sheets and blankets under the mattress. They'll be readily available when you need to change the sheets or to add a blanket in colder weather.

■ Store additional linens, including mattress pads used for fold-out couches, under the couch pillows.

■ Clean linens before storing them because stains and spots will set if left in the fabric. But do not spray starch on them because it will cause the fabric to yellow! Store linens in a dry place so they won't mildew or acquire a musty smell.

■ Attach wire baskets under linen closet shelves, if there's room. Use them to store sachets, soaps, or smaller items.

Classic Hint

Before rearranging your linen closet, ask yourself what you use the most: sheets, towels, or linens? Are your sheets on the most convenient shelf? Are your towels too high for the kids to reach? Are the washcloths separated from the towels? Where are the special-occasion tablecloths? The pillowcases?

Place bath towels, hand towels, and washcloths in the most convenient spot in your linen closet—about waist level, so children can get them easily. Place the sheets and pillowcases on the shelf above the towels. On the top shelves, put odds and ends such as fancy guest towels, tablecloths, and place mats that are not used daily.

Coat Closets

■ Place a coatrack in the hall for wet clothes to dry out before they go back into the closet.

■ Create a designated location for family members to store their outdoor gear near the entryway. Set up a small table to hold keys, mail, etc., with pegs or hooks hanging above it for hats, scarves, and light jackets. Or assign a different colored milk crate for each child's things.

■ Hang a rack with small hooks inside the front closet for all household keys, so you will always know where they are.

- Have lots of hats, mittens, and gloves to store? Use spring-action clothespins to clip them to hooks, a chain, or a rope hung on the closet door.

- Find an alternative place other than the front closet to store out-of-season coats, gloves, and hats.

Keeping Keys Organized

I bet there isn't anyone who hasn't mislaid or lost keys at some point in their life. Yes, even me! Many years ago, the door key to my car had slid off the key ring and I was locked out. I had to call my father to come and rescue me. I now keep a single car door key in my purse.

A friend of mine lost her entire set of keys in her apartment. She swore she had put them on the couch, but when she had to leave for an important meeting, they were nowhere to be found. After searching for 45 minutes and being late to the meeting, she found the keys had fallen into the couch coils.

Later that day she went out and bought a beautiful basket to place on a table at her front door, and to this day she drops her keys into it every time she comes home. She has never lost them since.

These key ideas may assist you in keeping yours organized:

- Have one central place for hanging all keys. Or place keys in a bowl or basket or on a rack near the front or back door.

- Put keys on or near anything you need to remember to take or to check, so you won't leave home without them! For example, hang or place them in the kitchen near the coffeepot or close to your briefcase or purse.

- If you don't want to take a whole key chain, simply use a large safety pin to secure a door key to the band of your skirt or pants or inside a jacket.

- Give teens their own set of keys to the family cars when they start driving.

- Color-code keys or key chains for each family member.

- Trace new keys on a sheet of paper and keep it in your household files. Then you will have a pattern to match when you have to figure out exactly what that mystery key is.

- Those who have a "very safe" place to hide a key outside the door should do so, but don't tell anyone except when needed. It may save you a big locksmith bill!

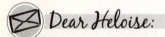 *Dear Heloise:*

My husband and I got tired of trying to remember where things are stored in our home, so we inventoried every closet in the house. We listed the items on each shelf and posted the list in a conspicuous place in the closet, to be seen when the closet is opened. The main closet of the house contains an alphabetized master list of all items in all closets. Next to each item on this master list, we posted a code showing which closet the item was in and which shelf it was on. A "warning" sign in each closet reads, "If you permanently remove or add anything to this closet, amend the closet index and master list." No more lost objects!

Dear Reader: Now this it the ultimate in closet organizing! For most of us, any version of making a general inventory or list can be helpful.

4

Bathrooms and the Laundry Room

Bathrooms

Because bathrooms get so much use on a daily basis, they can become a clutter catastrophe. Clutter multiplies in this small space, thanks to tons of cosmetics and hair, bath, and cleaning products. Enlist all members of your family in helping to keep order in this room. Here are a few helpful rules for the bathroom:

- *Nothing is left on the floor.* Everyone must hang up towels and clothes.

- *If you use it, clean it.* Everyone puts the caps back on products they use and wipes off the sink and counters.

- *Right stuff in the right place.* Everyone puts objects back in the drawers or cabinets where they found them.

To make following the bathroom rules easier, assign each family member one specific task in the bathroom. Keep several plastic bags in the bottom of the wastebasket, and a roll of paper towels, sponges, and a spray bottle filled with vinegar and water in a plastic bucket under the sink. Show family members how to use these products!

5-Minutes or 5-Things

In five minutes, you can:

- Hang up towels
- Wipe the mirror and sink clean
- Cull old cosmetics
- Arrange a shower caddy
- Clean out a vanity drawer

Five things to throw away:

- Expired medicines
- Soap slivers
- Old makeup
- Nearly empty bottles
- Dried out nail polish

- Place a clothes hamper for dirty clothes in the bathroom. If there's room, have one for whites and one for colors.

- Put several revolving trays into under-sink cabinets for easy access and organization.

- Install shelves over the toilet. They can hold towels or other bathroom accessories.

- Hook shower shelves over the showerhead or stick a caddie with suction cups on the shower wall. Hang a three-tier wire basket in the shower for the items you use daily.

- Use a shoe bag as extra storage for beauty products. Hang a hook over the bathroom door.

- Hang a wicker basket, beaded planter, or wire mesh baskets from the ceiling to hold toothpaste, brushes, combs, or anything else that clutters your counters. If there's no room to hang anything, keep a wicker basket in the under-sink cabinet to hold countertop items until they are needed.

- Attach pretty baskets to a wall to hold hair accessories.

- Put divider inserts in bathroom drawers to keep all the small stuff organized.

- Keep a squeegee in the shower for quick tile and glass door cleanup.

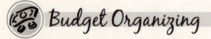 *Budget Organizing*

- Reuse tall potato chip cans as cover-up containers. Decorate the can with adhesive paper or paint to match your bathroom décor.

Slip it over hair spray, room deodorizer, or other unattractive items on your vanity.

▪ Don't throw out the small, square, decorative tissue boxes when empty. Instead, store cotton balls inside, or reuse as a dispenser for disposable plastic gloves.

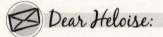 *Dear Heloise:*

This bit of advice is for the gals who have trouble keeping their cosmetics in order. I bought a small fishing-tackle box—the kind that, when opened, has two trays that automatically rise up to greet you. There are so many nice compartments and it's just perfect for storing all kinds of tubes, mascara, eye shadows, etc. In the bottom of the box, I store creams, powder, perfume, and deodorant.

Dear Reader: These boxes are not just for men anymore. Plus, you can just toss in your toothpaste and medication, and you'll be ready for any trip. Just hope your husband doesn't accidentally grab it for his fishing trip!

Dear Heloise:

I have always looked for a way to keep my cosmetics together on my vanity table and at the same time make it easy to pick them up and put them back quickly. The solution to my problem was to buy a space-saving turntable at the local hardware store. It spins so all my makeup and perfume are always right at my fingertips.

Dear Reader: I do the same and use them for all my nail polishes and bottles of lotion, too.

Medicine Chest

Organize the bathroom medicine chest at least once a year. Place items used daily such as toothpaste and mouthwash on lower shelves, along with first-aid items like bandages, antiseptics, creams, and salves for easy access. Thermometers and cold and cough supplies belong on a higher shelf. Then discard the following:

- Expired medications

- Smashed, cracked, or discolored tablets or capsules

- Capsules that are soft or stuck together

- Aspirin tablets if they smell like vinegar—it's a sign they may be deteriorating

- Liquid medicine that has separated

- Bottles missing labels

Arrange medications so the labels can be read easily, and store them in a cool, dry place out of the reach of children. Never place medicines near insect repellent or mothballs; the vapors could be absorbed.

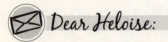 Dear Heloise:

I kept my vitamins above the kitchen sink along with my three dogs' heartworm medication. One morning I forgot to put on my glasses and took the heartworm pills by mistake! I didn't know whether to call the vet or my doctor. I called the vet and learned I wasn't in any danger. (My husband noted that I was fine, but just barking a lot!)

Dear Reader: Store these medications separately!

Dear Heloise:

I had to take several pills after an injury, including sleep medication. One day at work I grabbed the wrong bottle and took a sleeping pill. I nodded off at my desk, not realizing what I had done!

Dear Reader: Keep pills separated in a container that notes days and times. In this case, marking the sleeping pill bottle with a red X would have gotten your attention. Or draw a crescent moon on night medications and a smiley face for day meds.

Laundry Room

Give every member of your family a guided tour of the laundry room. Teach them how to do the laundry and what products to use to get their clothes clean. Explain the difference between detergent, bleach, and fabric softener, for example. Keep a sign posted with basic instructions.

- Often, laundry rooms are so small that space is a precious commodity. Install shelves above the machines to hold laundry products.

- If you do have the space, set up a counter for sorting and folding clothes as soon as they come out of the dryer.

- Keep garment racks, clothing trees, an iron, ironing board, and a laundry cart nearby.

- Hang a few small plastic bins or receptacles on the wall to hold a sewing kit (complete with pre-threaded needles and buttons) and lost-and-found items.

- Store all washing supplies in a large plastic basket in a cabinet or on a shelf so you have everything you need close at hand (and to keep any spills contained).

- Keep a notepad with a pen on a bulletin board near your laundry area. This is handy for jotting down the laundry products you need as you run out of them. It's also a good place to leave laundering instructions for family members.

- If you are waiting for the washer or dryer to stop, use the time to organize. Open any cabinet and reach way in the back to pull out and get rid of five items, such as empty boxes, bottles with a little cleaning stuff left, lint, odd socks, or old rags.

- Toss a load of laundry in the washing machine before you leave for work—minus water and soap. Whoever gets home first adds the detergent (and bleach if required) and pushes start. (*Caution:* Do not start the washer, dryer, or dishwasher and then leave the house!) Before dinner is on the table, the clean clothes are ready to go into the dryer. A load of clothes can be done each day, so it doesn't build up to a huge task over the weekend.

Heloise's Laundry List

Keep copies of this list on the laundry room door, and check off items to add to your weekly shopping list.

- ☐ Bleach
- ☐ Bluing
- ☐ Detergent
- ☐ Detergent booster
- ☐ Disinfectant
- ☐ Dryer sheets
- ☐ Enzyme presoaks

- ☐ Fabric finishes
- ☐ Fabric softener
- ☐ Fabric washes for delicates
- ☐ Pre-wash stain removers
- ☐ Sizing
- ☐ Starch
- ☐ Water softeners

Sorting

When it comes to sorting laundry, it helps to have a number of baskets on hand. You can also have receptacles just for towels or heavily soiled work clothes. Of course, the number of bins you set up depends on how much space you have.

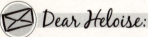 Dear Heloise:

Our family of five used to toss our laundry into one big central hamper with everything mixed together. This made it difficult to do a quick load of laundry because the whole pile had to be sorted. So we purchased three inexpensive plastic hampers in different colors. We gave the kids a little clothes-sorting lesson, and before long, we were all throwing our darks into a blue hamper, whites into a white hamper, and mixed colors into a beige hamper. Now all we do is grab a hamper and throw the clothes in the washer.

- Always separate light-colored garments from dark ones.

- Separate lint-producing garments like bath towels from lint-collecting ones such as synthetic or permanent-press clothes.

- Use a hamper only for big items like towels and jeans, and a small laundry bag for the small stuff like T-shirts.

- Buy some light-colored duffel bags and several indelible pens. Write washing instructions—hot, warm, and cold water—on the front of each laundry bag with the pen. Clothes can be put in the appropriate bag.

As we know too well, dark socks all look similar in color when you are trying to match them—and there always seems to be one without a mate! Here are several ways to keep them together:

- Pin socks in pairs with a nonrusting pin or hold them together with a plastic hook.

- Buy fabric paint pens. Match up black socks and label them with a letter and pairs of navy socks with a number. Each family member could have a label with different pen color.

- Presort colored socks before washing and place each "color" in its own zippered mesh lingerie bag.

 **Classic Hint**

Make about a half-dozen laundry bags out of nylon net (available at sewing and fabric stores). Label each bag or the hook you hang it on: whites, darks, pastels, delicates, towels—whatever laundry categories are appropriate for your family. Then place things in

their respective bags as they are used. When the bag is filled, you have a load for the washer.

Washing and Drying

- Read the care labels, detergent labels, and washer and dryer settings first!

- Check for fresh and old stains. Read the care labels on the clothing. Determine what the stain is and how to treat it before tossing into the machine.

- Empty pockets, close zippers and snaps before washing.

- Put the right amount of detergent into the machine first and not on top of the clothes.

- After the water and detergent have mixed, put clothing into the washing machine piece by piece. Lay each garment in a circle around the agitator.

- Set the washing machine on the correct water temperature and water level for the clothing and turn on.

- Turn the dryer on the correct setting for the fabric and dry.

- Do not use bleach on acetates, silk, spandex, or wool.

- Do not overload a washer or dryer because clothes will not get clean or dry properly. Never add wet items to a partially dried load.

- When you hang clothes immediately after pulling them out from the dryer, they may not have to be ironed later. Place a hook over the door and keep hangers on it, hang a clothesline, or use a foldable clothes rack.

Putting Away Laundry

- To cut down on time sorting and folding socks, fold them right as you take them off the line or out of the dryer.

- After folding clothes (especially towels, sheets, underwear, and T-shirts), place them *under* an existing stack in your drawer or shelf so they will be rotated evenly and the same ones won't be used constantly. This will help the items last longer.

- If you have a big household, color-code clothing. Assign each person a different color, and dot the care label or the waist seam of undergarments. That will make identification easier.

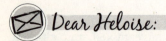 *Dear Heloise:*

While folding laundry, I fold the bras and undies together to make sure I have five sets. That way I'm set for work for the whole week.

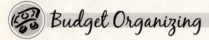 *Budget Organizing*

Recycle the large plastic caps from fabric softener or liquid detergent bottles. They can be used to:

- Store tubes of lipstick or small makeup brushes

- Sort screws and nuts at your workbench

- Use for mixing small amounts of craft paint

Organizing Sewing Supplies

- Store sewing machine bobbins in cleaned, empty prescription bottles.

- Use large plastic storage bags to hold all the pieces you have cut from a pattern, including the instructions and notions for each project.

- Keep empty thread spools because you can use them to wrap decorative lace, rickrack, or trimming. Secure with a straight pin.

- Buy an inexpensive fishing-tackle box to hold all sewing notions. All those compartments will hold everything from pins to buttons.

- Utilize a plain bar of soap as a pincushion. Keep the wrapper on and insert pins and needles. Being coated with soap will make pins slide more easily through fabric.

- Another great "pincushion" is a magnet. It's really handy if you've spilled straight pins. Just swipe over the surface, and pins will stick to it.

5

The Garage, Attic, and Basement

Garage

Most garages seem to end up as *the* place to dump or store everything in a most disorderly way. If your garage looks like a tornado has hit it or it's holding everything except the car, it's time to clean it up and organize all the contents. Use the A-B-C method to sort and toss anything you don't use or need. Then organize what's left.

Divide everything either by season—summer, winter, fall, and spring—or by category—sports equipment, Christmas decorations, gardening equipment, car repair, etc. Install hanging racks, hooks, Peg-Boards, and shelves. Use clearly marked containers to corral loose items. And remember, *right stuff in the right place*. Never allow items, such as bikes or rakes, to be left on the floor where people could trip and injure themselves. Always keep the garbage cans, lawn mowers, and/or snow blowers in the same place. In the summer, keep gardening tools and summer equipment in easy reach. Swap them with your shovels and de-icers in the winter.

- Keep like items together, such as carpentry tools or gardening tools, paint containers, and car items.

- Label items that are stored in boxes or unmarked containers. Containers that are stacked high should be secured well so they cannot fall on top of anyone. (Do not stack cardboard boxes too high as they tend to weaken and collapse over time.)

- Use air space by hanging a hammock to store things like holiday decorations or other seasonal items.

- Store cans of paint (first put a swipe of the paint color on the outside of the can for identification), pesticides, gas, or other potentially dangerous items separately in one special, secure area. Label them clearly.

- Get utility racks designed specifically for rakes, weed trimmers, shovels, sports equipment, and bikes, so they can't fall over and become a dangerous hazard.

- Put sports equipment for each season in separate, labeled containers or hang them from heavy-duty hooks in one area.

- Rolling carts can be useful to hold seasonal items that may need to be moved around, or for tires and car gear.

- Store patio or deck supplies in heavy-duty cardboard or plastic boxes.

- Separate grill accessories into one area or bin for easy access.

- Lay seldom-used or seasonal items, like storm windows or screens, on a platform or shelving across ceiling joists in the garage. Prepare a log or map of where these items are located.

- To make moving and taking out garbage less of a heavy pain, purchase cans with wheels. There are many durable and inexpensive kinds available at supermarkets, hardware or home improvement stores.

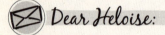 *Dear Heloise:*

Our Peg-Board in the garage is always getting disorganized by the re-hanging of the rakes, shovels, tools, brooms, etc. in the wrong place. One day, after my husband organized it perfectly, he got the bright idea to take a picture of it. He hung the picture right next to the Peg-Board. Now we know where everything belongs by just looking at the picture.

Dear Reader: A picture is worth a thousand tools! Alternatively you could paint the outline of each object onto the Peg-Board so there's no question of where each item goes—and you'll know instantly what things are missing!

Tools

- Save glass jars of all sizes to hold all those small tools and items—nuts, bolts, screws, blades, etc. so you will be able to see what you need. You can also nail the metal lids of glass jars underneath shelves. You'll save space and never lose the lids!

- Use coffee cans for storing small tools.

- To protect expensive tools, get a metal toolbox; this will help prevent moisture from rusting them.

- Put shovels, rakes, and hoes into a big garbage can with wheels. Hang small gardening tools on S hooks around the rim. Just pull the whole can to the garden area you are working.

- Wrap garden hose around a sturdy wooden coat hanger and then hang it on a hook in the garage.

Protecting Your Car

- Put reflector tape on any objects that might be in your way at night, particularly if you don't have good lighting in the garage.

- Hang a tennis ball in the center of your garage parking space. It will be the guide for parking in the center of the designated space.

- If you back into the garage, hang on old tire at bumper height to protect the wall and your car!

- Recycle old inner tubes, carpet scraps, or rubber mats. Use them to pad anything that might come in contact with your car.

- Use fluorescent spray paint to outline parking spaces for cars on the garage floor. You can also do this for bicycles or even garbage cans!

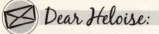

Dear Heloise:

I found a way to make my children put things back where they belong and keep the garage in a halfway-straightened fashion. I made a chart and outlined the area where items are to be kept. The lawn mower and children's bicycles even have a place. If I go into the garage and something is not where it belongs, I write the item down and whichever child put it there has to pay a fine. We start with a nickel, and each time they have something in the wrong place, the fine goes up!

Dear Reader: A wonderful way for your kids to learn about organization and money at the same time.

Attic and Basement

An attic can be an extremely useful place to store family treasures, so don't let it become a nightmare where things are dumped rather than dealt with. If you're not even sure what's in your attic, now is the time to clean it out and get it organized! Schedule a weekend to tackle it. Establish order in the attic by creating "zones" for different items—holiday items in one area, clothing in another, etc. (Be sure to label all boxes clearly.) Attics are often prone to dampness and pests, so it's crucial to properly store items in this area.

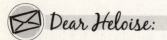

Dear Heloise:

I am an attic fanatic and am constantly storing things there. I stapled a self-sealing bag to the attic door with a list in it of the items

in the attic. This saves a lot of digging when I need something that "I know I put up there."

Just because the basement is out of sight doesn't mean it shouldn't be organized. Because heating and hot water units are usually there, keeping this area neat is even more important for safety reasons. Don't store paint or other flammables in the basement. Clutter can catch fire, so get rid of everything you are not using. Basements often flood, so don't store anything valuable there if you have this problem.

Dampness in the basement causes a musty smell and mildew to thrive. Use activated charcoal, an effective absorbent, to keep the basement as dry as possible and promote good air circulation. Activated charcoal is available at pet supply, aquarium, or large home improvement stores. Put it in open containers in the areas that need it the most, or place the charcoal in old panty hose and hang in a corner (where you can't hit your head)!

- Keep a flashlight and a pair of kneepads handy at the entrance to attics. Create a clear walkway or crawl space through your organized boxes so you can easily find what you're looking for. Don't allow items to fall over or block it.

- Store out-of-season clothes in sealed plastic bins or decorations in large trash bags. Label bags and boxes clearly.

- Clean the attic and basement at least once a year. Check the attic for mice or squirrel invasions; check the basement for pests. Get rid of dust and dirt.

- You don't want a fire hazard! Toss out any paper or other flammable items.

Storing Holiday Decorations

- Wrap tinsel garlands and tree lights around empty cardboard gift-wrap tubes. This will keep them tangle free.

- Use egg cartons to store small ornaments. Glass, fragile, or favorite ornaments should be wrapped separately with newspaper or tissue paper. Liquor boxes that are segmented are great for ornaments.

- Use large popcorn tins to store rolls of gift wrap, garlands, extension cords, holiday lights, or decorations.

- Store heavy items in the bottoms of boxes and light or fragile items on the top to prevent breakage.

- Put an artificial tree into the storage area last so you can take it out first. Keep it in a cool dry place.

- Label holiday boxes and store them according to the first-in, last-out system.

- Toss used fabric softener sheets into storage boxes before sealing them up. This will help to prevent a musty smell that often lurks in garages, basements, and attics.

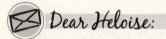 Dear Heloise:

When storing boxes in the attic or basement, number each box with a permanent marker. Then number an index card and list and label what each box contains. Tape the cards on the back of the door to the attic or storage room. This saves time when you go to look for some particular things in storage.

Dear Reader: A great idea. And you'll want to label every box with the contents just in case your master list goes astray!

5-Minutes or 5-Things

In five minutes, you can:

- Make a "zone" map for the attic
- Paint a "parking space" on your garage floor for your car
- Fill a trash can with garage or basement junk
- Pick up your tools and put them where they belong
- Hang a Peg-Board

Five things to throw away:

- Broken tools
- Moth-eaten clothing
- Empty boxes
- Near-empty cans of paint
- Any unearthed items last seen in the 1970s!

PART TWO

Keeping Your Family Organized

6

Kids' Stuff

Keeping a family organized can be a full-time job! Kids' lives are a whirlwind of activities, friends, play dates, sleepovers, and sports—not to mention the time it takes to prepare meals and keep clothes, personal, and school things in order. It's an amazing task, but most moms do it and do it well! Being a home juggler is part of the family circus.

You can make your job easier by teaching your children basic organizational skills. Teach them how to *use it or lose it* and always put *the right stuff in the right place*. Walk them around their room and point out items that don't adhere to the rules. One way to reinforce this skill is to make organizing a game. For example, you might have a pick-up contest. See who can pick up and put away their toys and clothes the fastest. The winner gets a prize. And the loser gets a big hug!

Kids' Rooms

Let's face it, they're usually a mess! *Organizing* is usually not in a child's or teen's vocabulary. Getting children to organize their belongings can be a difficult and time-consuming task, but it can be done.

Try to provide your kids with plenty of storage solutions for their stuff. Let them pick out cool bins or stackables. Allowances and rewards for hanging up clothes, cleaning, and organizing their room may influence them. Eventually they will get it!

Fun Storage Solutions

Make organizing fun for your kids by having them transform ordinary household items into works of art—that double as storage bins!

- Start with a clean gallon milk jug. Cut off the top at an angle, making sure there are no sharp edges. Kids can decorate the jugs with markers. These are perfect containers to store toys, and with the handles, they can also be hung on hooks.

- Reuse coffee cans or other cans with plastic lids to hold crayons and other art supplies. Kids can decorate the outside of the can with construction paper and ribbon.

- Save small metal bandage boxes to hold crayons—they're a perfect fit. Kids can paint these tins their favorite color.

- Empty margarine tubs can hold marbles or small toys, or be used as a water receptacle for a child's watercolors.

■ Cover a large cardboard box with fabric or wallpaper for an inexpensive but personalized toy box.

■ Save large, 46-ounce juice cans. Cut off one end, making certain there are no sharp edges. Paint them, arrange on their sides, and glue the cans together. The cans make round cubbyholes, which can be hung on your child's wall or placed on a shelf. This storage unit is a great way to hold and organize small toy collections.

Dear Heloise:

I keep puzzles organized by writing a letter on the back of each piece. I assign each puzzle a different letter, so that if pieces from different puzzles get mixed up, it's no big deal.

Toys

■ Decorate plastic trash cans with your children's favorite decals for storing toys and other items in their rooms.

■ Use laundry baskets to hold toys. They're easy to pull around the room for collecting.

■ Clean out round ice-cream cartons and use to store small toys. Many have plastic windows on top so your child can keep track of what's inside.

■ Hang a hammock from the ceiling of your child's room and fill it with stuffed toys or lightweight sports equipment.

■ Use a clean, dry, low-sided kiddie wading pool to store toys or building blocks. It can slide under kids' beds.

- Divide a very young child's toys into groups. For example, separate toys into a bag for each day of the week. This way, they will always have "new" toys to play with. (Remember to put them away when they are finished playing!)

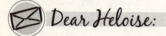 *Dear Heloise:*

I have my children go through all their toys right before the holidays. We discard broken ones, we keep the ones they still play with, and others are donated to a local children's home before they write their own "wish list."

Clothing

- Give each child a distinctive color laundry basket for their room to hold their dirty clothes inside. When the laundry is done, they can carry it back to their room and put their clothes away.

- For children who are just learning how to dress or who have a hard time deciding what to wear, use this method: Place matching shirts and pants with socks and underwear on one hanger. Let them choose the outfit they want to wear, rather than the individual articles. Your child won't come downstairs in a clown outfit!

- Arrange matching clothing/outfits in large see-through zipper-type plastic bags in children's dresser drawers. They can pull out a bag and get dressed in a hurry.

- Label each drawer or paste a photo on it so they know what's inside.

- If your kids share a closet, label the tags on their clothes and shoes with initials so they can quickly identify what's theirs.

Dear Heloise:

I solved the problem of putting away my teenagers' laundry. I deliberately placed T-shirts and underwear in the wrong drawers for several weeks. My kids finally said they wanted to put their own clothes away.

Dear Heloise:

After the birth of my grandson, I was trying to sort out all of the new little outfits. As they were all different sizes, I was having a hard time keeping them separated. I came up with this solution: I cut round disks out of plastic margarine tops (three inches in diameter), then cut a circle the size of the closet rod out of the middle. I wrote the different sizes on the circle with the hole in it and slipped it over the closet rod.

Budget Organizing

- Don't throw out an outgrown plastic infant bathtub! Instead use it as a portable toy box or small pet bathtub.

- Use an old footlocker for storage in an older child's room. It can hold skates and sporting goods. To do double-duty as an extra seat, simply put a long pillow on top.

Busy Schedules

From sports practice to scouting to dance lessons, children often have busier schedules than their parents. Help organize your children's activities with a big calendar with large squares for every day. Use a different color pen to write in each child's activities. Then there's no confusion about who has to be where and when. (I like those "washable" calendars so as dates and times change, you can wipe off the old and write in the new!)

If getting ready for school in the mornings is a hassle, set up a daily routine for your kids. Before bedtime, have kids find everything they need for school the next day—locate homework assignments and permission slips, pick out their clothes, even decide what they will eat for lunch. Moms tell me that sticking to this routine really makes mornings less stressful.

- Teach your children how to make their own breakfasts and lunches. Let them choose, within reason, what they want to eat and to pack for school lunches. Most important—show them how to clean up afterward!

- Make a week's worth of lunches over the weekend. In an assembly line, place out bread, meat, or cheese and put sandwiches together, but don't add mayo or mustard. Freeze them in resealable plastic bags. Pull one out each weekday. They will thaw by lunch!

- Keep a basket by the front door for kids' papers that need a parent's signature and to be returned to school. Check it every day in the evenings and again as kids leave for school.

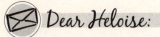 *Dear Heloise:*

I use a three-ring binder to organize our sports and other extracurricular-activity information. I label a divider for each sport or activity. If more than one child participates in the same sport, I use a different divider for each of their teams. I keep rosters, schedules, field directions, and coaches' letters in each section. This way we have all our information organized and easily accessible.

Dear Reader: Wow! This cuts down on family stress and could be used for school and classroom information, too.

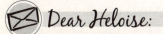 *Dear Heloise:*

Here's a hint for storing all the papers and artwork that the kids bring home. I bought a jumbo-size plastic storage bin for each of my kids and labeled them with their names. As the papers come home they all get displayed on the refrigerator for a week, then stored away in their own bins, which I keep in the laundry room. By the end of the school year, the bins are filled to the top. We pick a day to sort through the bins and decide which papers to keep. We usually narrow the pile down to about one-tenth of its original size. From there, the keepers go into a large envelope that is labeled with the year and stored in the kids' closets.

Dear Reader: Those school papers can really pile up, and it's hard to part with them, but your system makes it easy to save the most memorable ones.

When Kids Get Sick

Coping with a sick child (or two!) becomes easier if you can stay organized. Be sure to maintain a calendar for doctor appointments and keep folders for medical papers.

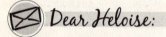 *Dear Heloise:*

When marking doctor appointments on our calendar, I write the time and circle the date with colored markers. I use a different color for each family member. It's great for when I have to check back or ahead for an appointment.

■ Put a revolving tray on the nightstand to hold medicine, tissues, a glass of water, an alarm clock—anything the patient (and you, the nurse) will need at hand.

■ Organize a bedside table or tables with everything you think your family member will use—heating pad, hot water bottle, thermometer, and vaporizer. If you don't have a table, use an adjustable ironing board.

■ For a young child, keep a potty chair next to the bed overnight.

■ Serve your child's food in a muffin tin. It will help prevent spills in the bed.

■ Make a "fun box" for a sick child. Put crayons, drawing paper, coloring books, card games, favorite toys, CDs, or electronic games in it. Your child will have activities to keep him or her from getting bored.

■ To keep hot drinks hot and cold drinks cold, fill a thermos in the morning with a favorite drink and put it by the patient's bed.

Dear Heloise:

Since both my husband and I work, mornings are terribly hectic and rushed. I could never get ahead and was always running late. One weekend I sat down and compiled a list of ways that I can get better organized in the mornings. Here are some of the most successful ideas:

Breakfast was my worst chore, so before going to bed I set the table with all the bowls, plates, silverware, and glasses. I also set all nonperishable items like cereal or donuts on the table. I did this for the first week, but now I assign each family member a turn at setting the table.

I have everyone decide on Friday what they will wear the entire next week. This way I don't have to do laundry through the week and no one is whining, "What am I going to wear?" I also can do any necessary mending or ironing over the weekend.

My youngest child goes to day care, so I fix his diaper bag the night before. I fill all his bottles with formula and place them in the refrigerator. In the morning, all I need to do is put the bottles in the diaper bag and I'm ready to go.

I organize my briefcase at night, place any papers or supplies I may need for the coming day in it, and put it by the front door so all I have to do is grab it on the way out.

Last, I make a list of telephone numbers for baby-sitters I may need in case of an emergency or a child's illness and place it by the telephone.

Now my mornings actually run smoothly!

7

Pets

Many of us consider our pets important family members. Just like everyone else, their lives need to be organized, too!

When you get a pet, decide who is going to be the major caregiver in your family and who will help. The responsibility shouldn't fall on just one person's shoulders. Assign specific care tasks to each family member. Children who want pets have to learn how to take care of them, too. It's a good lesson in responsibility.

- When you bring home new puppies and kittens, protect them from possible harmful situations as you would a child. Don't leave poisonous plants in their reach. Don't let them wander near a swimming pool unattended.

- Keep pets out of your home office or any room where there are lots of cords that can be chewed on.

- Contain excitable animals at night so they are not roaming around the house, getting into trouble.

- When you are going on vacation, plan well in advance for qualified pet-sitters or well-run kennels.

- Leave behind a will or instructions for family and friends so they know your wishes for your pets in case of an accident, disability, or death.

Keeping Your Pet Organized

Set a daily schedule for your pet. Make sure it's fed on time, that its bedding or cage is cleaned regularly, and that it's walked when it needs to be. Try not to allow your family to overindulge your animal in the food department or let it develop bad habits like sleeping where it's not supposed to. Taking a pet to training courses can be helpful in establishing discipline.

Give your pets their own calendar so it's easy for you to schedule veterinarian appointments, activity dates, grooming sessions, and dates when they will need someone else to care for them. Or consistently used a colored marker to write pet appointments on your household's master calendar.

Planning a Diet

All family members need to know exactly what their pet should eat and when. They also should know what could happen if the pet eats something it shouldn't. Talk to your veterinarian annually about what kind of diet your pet needs.

- Feed your pet at the same time every day, perhaps when you eat breakfast or dinner.

- Ask your vet if it's all right to vary your pet's diet, and the correct way to do so.

- Find out if your pet is overweight and the proper amount of food you should be feeding it.

- Buy pet food in bulk when it's on sale, but don't scrimp on the quality. If you switch to a cheaper brand, make sure it's equally as nutritious for your animal.

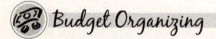 *Budget Organizing*

Reuse plastic containers, such as those for margarine or yogurt, as scoops for dry pet food.

Health Care

- Try to keep all your pets' medications in one area, away from your family's medications. I like to use a wicker basket.

- Give them the pills at the same time every day or as indicated.

- Post your veterinarian's number prominently. In case of an emergency, every family member needs to know how to get in touch with the vet and animal poison control.

- Keep a file with your pet's vaccination and registration information, along with medical history, etc.

- Keep an annual calendar to mark when they may need immunizations, booster shots, and checkups.

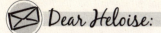 Dear Heloise:

I find it helpful to take a copy of my dog's health and shot records to the kennel to keep on file when I board my dog. I also carry a copy with me just in case. This way in an emergency, another vet knows my dog's medical history.

Schedule Time for Exercise

Like you, your dog and even your cat need exercise. Try to plan it around your family activities on a regular basis.

- Take your dog on your normal walk or run.

- Have a fenced-in area where your pet can run and play freely.

- Let your children play with animals during their own regular play time.

- Don't walk or run a newly groomed animal during the hours of peak sunshine; its skin could become burned.

- During summer, exercise your pet early in the morning or after sunset. The hot sun can cause heat exhaustion.

- During winter, wash off your dog's feet after exercise. Salt or chemical de-icers could irritate their pads.

Dear Heloise:

When the cats or dog have to go outside on cold days, I always set my kitchen timer for three to four minutes. It's so easy to get busy and forget they are out.

Dear Reader: A timely hint. I had a friend who went to her neighbor's house for a party in the middle of winter. The dog was let out in the yard and everyone, including the owner, forgot it was outside. An hour later, an angry, chilled dog was let in. Don't ever leave your furry friends out in the cold.

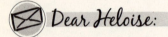 *Dear Heloise:*

Each year when it was time to change my dog's rabies tag, I always had trouble putting it on his collar. The S hook was hard to close so I solved the problem by putting the tag on a circular key ring. Now, all I do is slip the key ring on his collar.

Storing Pet Supplies

- Use a clean plastic or metal garbage can with a lid to store any large bags of dry pet food. Put a scoop inside, and keep the lid on securely to protect it from bugs or rodents. Store food in the garage or pantry.

- Store pet food in a decorative way by keeping it in a large empty tin.

- Re-use plastic take-out food containers with lids to hold canned pet food. Keep several pre-measured meals in the fridge. At mealtime, just pop off the lid and serve.

- Collect playthings in a laundry basket, shopping bag, cardboard box, or wire mesh basket.

- Hang leashes on a hook near an outside door.

■ Label all your pet's bowls, toys, grooming supplies, and medicines so they don't get misused.

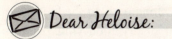 *Dear Heloise:*

We keep a basket in the den for all of the puppies' toys. This way, their toys are accessible to them and in an attractive container. Rawhide bones and stuffed toys alike are tossed into the basket for the dogs to drag out again.

Dear Reader: We do the same for Cabbie, our Miniature Schnauzer. Not only are the toys organized all in one place, but the dog gets a little exercise, too.

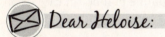 *Dear Heloise:*

You don't have to spend a lot of money on a bed for your cat. I made one for a couple of dollars. I bought a plastic crate used for storage and put an old bed pillow on the bottom. My cat, Roxy, loves it.

Dear Reader: Cats love to curl up in just about anything, from wicker baskets to trays. Your suggestion gives us an inexpensive way to keep a kitty happy.

Traveling with Your Pet

If you plan to bring your pet along on a trip, be sure to check with the hotel or motel in advance to ensure that pets are accepted or that kennels are close by. Make advance plans for how you will care for your pet during a trip. If you are sightseeing, where will your pet be?

- Prepare a carrier for your pet, along with all the food your pet will need. Put the amount of dry food your pet eats each day in sealed plastic bags that you can keep in the car, along with a jug of water.

- Update your pet's ID tags and include another contact phone number aside from your home number. You won't be there to take a call!

- Make sure the collar or harness your pet wears is secure.

- Make a copy of your pet's medical records, and bring them along with your veterinarian's phone number in case of an emergency. Make sure shots are up to date.

- Never leave your pet in a car during hot weather. In less than 20 minutes, a car's interior temperature can rise to 120 degrees F—even if the temperature outside is only 85 degrees.

Boarding Your Pet

Leaving your pet when you go away, whether for a weekend or a month, is an important decision. Give yourself plenty of time before you go on a vacation or business trip to find a good facility or pet-sitter.

- Research kennels carefully. Do not shop by phone. Go to the kennel and check it out. Many of the costs relate to the pet's size and also what kind of a kennel it is. Get recommendations from a vet or family and friends who are happy with the services provided.

- The boarding facility should be clean and well lit. It should be relatively free from odors. It should insist on current booster immunizations. Ask what the policies are for emergencies. Watch the people who are caring for the pets—are they comfortable with them?

- If you are not satisfied with kennels in your area, you may want to hire a bonded pet-sitter. They charge by the day and will visit your pet. Or you might leave your pet with a trusted neighbor or friend. Either way, leave them all the important emergency information: where they can reach you, a neighbor's phone number, emergency vet number, written information on pet's medications, eating and living habits.

Dear Heloise:

We have four dogs, and when we travel with them or board them, I bag their dry food in pre-measured snack bags. Each bag has a dog's name on it, and at feeding time, all that needs to be done is to match the bags with the dog. I save the bags for re-use for the next time we travel.

If Your Pet Is Lost

- Make a flyer with your pet's name, picture, identifying marks, and your phone number.

- Call local animal organizations and vets. Go to shelters and give them the flyer.

- Let your neighbors know your pet is missing. Put up signs all around the neighborhood and be sure to include your phone number.

- Drive around your area and look up and down the streets. Post your flyers in local businesses.

- Place a lost-pet notice in the newspaper with your pet's description and your contact information.

- Go online. You can post a lost-pet ad and photo. Many local communities have these sites.

8

Personal Organizing

Even with all the incredible new technology available in our homes—cell phones, fax machines, Internet—we still are awash in a sea of paper clutter. From our children's school reports to letters from friends, from electric bills to dry-cleaning receipts, paper is everywhere!

The problem with paper is that you can accumulate so much, and eventually you are buried in an unsightly avalanche of the stuff. Try to handle each piece only once. Open your junk mail, and if it does not seem appealing, throw it out. Read your bills and immediately put them into the system you have for paying them (see A System for Bill Paying, page 102). Read personal letters and answer them, or put them where they will be answered on a designated letter-writing day. Don't print out e-mails unless absolutely necessary.

Use a shredder when you dispose of all personal documents—credit card bills, solicitations, or anything with your personal information on it. Identity theft is a serious problem, and you don't want to be a victim of it.

5-Minutes or 5-Things

In five minutes, you can:

- Record several personal contacts in an address book
- Pay and file a bill
- Write a note to a friend
- Organize your desk drawer
- Sort paperwork

Five things to throw away:

- Old directories
- Unused or expired coupons
- Credit card solicitations
- Old catalogs and magazines
- Receipts you no longer need

Setting Up a Home Office

Whether or not you work out of your home, every home should have a designated "office space" for personal and financial affairs. Be it a full-size study or a small kitchen nook, it's important to design your home office for the person who's going to use it the most. My husband and I each have separate office spaces because we have different working and organizational styles.

- If you don't have a separate room, look for a small space where you could put a built-in desk or fold-up table that could be enclosed so children and dogs can't get into it.

- Hide an office space behind a three-panel screen or big potted plant.

- Buy a filing cabinet to store papers. You can hide it with an attractive throw or some pretty material.

- Create an office space in a closet.

- Use the shelves in an armoire as office space. Some armoires have an office configuration already built in. When you're done working, close the doors and you have an attractive piece of furniture for the room.

- Buy a rolling desk system with cabinets. When your workday is over, roll it into a corner or closet.

- Place a "do not disturb" sign on the door. Let your children know what that means and what the rules are for entering.

Be Creative with Home Office Furniture

When setting up your space, you may be able to save a lot of money with clever storage solutions.

- Make a desk out of a pre-finished hollow-core door mounted on two file cabinets or sawhorses.

- Pull out the top drawer of a bedside table and place a writing surface on it for an impromptu desk.

- Create the old college-student-style bookcase with boards and bricks.

- Plastic milk crates can be used to store files. Just insert hanging files. Color-code the crates and stack them in a closet to hide away.

- Sturdy computer-paper boxes can also be used as a makeshift filing cabinet.

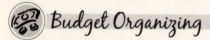 *Budget Organizing*

- Make desk trays out of old serving trays.

- Plastic film canisters are handy to hold change, stamps, or push pins.

- Don't throw out the plastic flats that hold nursery plants. When they're empty wash, rinse, and dry the trays. Use them as in and out baskets in your office.

- Staple a couple of yogurt cups together. Place them inside drawers to hold paper clips or tacks.

- Save cracked or chipped mugs to use as pencil holders.

Computers

- Be sure to keep your computer area organized—that means around it and inside it!

- Get appropriate organizing software for the work you do.

- Use electronic calendars. You can download many for free.

- Clean out the files (and e-mails) in your computer at least once a week. Like paper files, you want to clear out and delete unnecessary, old data that takes up room in your system.

- Store computer supplies—paper, cartridges, disks—in a specially designated drawer, in a box, or on a shelf.

- Organize pens, staples, and clips on your desk in attractive dishes or baskets.

- Get several cord organizers to bundle all those cords attached to your computer and office equipment. Not only will they keep cords from becoming a tangled mess, they also will make your space more attractive.

Budget Organizing

Create a standard cover sheet for all fax transmissions. Put it into a clear plastic sleeve, and write the sending information on the sleeve with dry erasable markers. When you're done transmitting, erase the marker with a blackboard eraser and the cover sheet is ready for the next transmission. You'll always be ready for faxing and will save money by not using a separate sheet of paper for each transmission.

Disks

- Label and index disks immediately after you've copied information onto them.

- Store disks in a caddie away from light, such as hot desk lamps and windowsills, and away from heat sources and vents.

- Do not keep disks in hot cars because they can warp or otherwise become damaged. If you have to travel with them, store in a disk carrier in a cooler.

- Be careful when transporting disks through an airport, because X rays may damage them. Instead, give them to the security guard to handle.

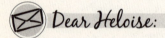 *Dear Heloise:*

At various times I see magazine or newspaper articles that give me ideas for special occasions, plans for remodeling the house, books I would like to read, vacation plans, and so forth. Rather than save the entire magazine or forget these fleeting ideas, I cut them out and put them into a binder. I also use index dividers to file these ideas alphabetically by topic. Now I can have all my ideas available quickly and easily. Sure cuts down on paper and magazine clutter.

Create a Personal Organizer

Maintaining all the family addresses, phone numbers, and e-mail addresses is a daunting task—not to mention keeping track of special occasions, appointments, and business contacts, too. It's crucial to have these items in your home office: an address book, a calendar, a notebook, and writing implements. You may also want to carry a pocket-size version of all these in your purse.

Everyone seems to have a personal organizer system that works for them. Some people love the new electronic organizers, others use the computer, and still others must have a paper system. It doesn't matter what type of organizers you use, as long as you use them! Here are my favorite personal organizing hints:

- Keep track of your addresses in a 3-by-5 index card file or Rolodex. It's easy to change information just by replacing cards! Add notes of birthdays, anniversaries, home or work phone numbers, and e-mail addresses, too. Relevant personal info can also go on these cards for a quick reference.

- Write information that may change in pencil.

- Staple or clip cards for doctor, hairdresser, or other appointments to your calendar. When you get home, write the next one in your calendar or enter the date in your electronic organizer—ASAP so you don't forget.

- Keep a small 3-by-5-inch memo book in your purse or pocket to write down whatever you need to remember. For example, if someone at a meeting asks you a question, you can call back with the answer—if you have written the question down and the person's phone number in the notebook. You can scribble the names of people you have just met or bits of information you might need in the future into the notebook, then you won't forget names and facts.

- Label notebooks with the dates they were used, such as

June–December, and then keep them so you'll have all sorts of phone numbers and information handy when you need it.

■ Spiral spelling-test notebooks, sold in stationery and office supply stores, are good for to-do lists. They are about half the width of a secretary's spiral pad and are lined and numbered.

■ When you are given business cards at various functions, write down on the back of the card the function, the date, spouse's name, and any other tips that identify the owner of the business card. Otherwise, you end up with a pile of business cards in a desk drawer that don't mean a thing to you. They also can be scanned into your computer.

■ Create files for everything: one for each child's school records, another for their doctor's info, along with all of yours. Keep files with directions to places you have difficulty finding. Once you get information you will use again, pop it into the right file. Of course you can create these files on your computer, too.

■ When you read a magazine or newspaper, tear out only the pages or articles you want and store them in a file folder or punch holes to put the pages into a ring binder. Or scan the articles into your computer. Either way, you will know where you can find it when you need it. Then you can toss or recycle the magazine or newspaper.

Remembering Occasions

Maintaining friendships and being there for those special people in your life takes time and energy—so a little organization never hurts. After all, you are the one who has to write notes or make phone calls. Here are some easy ways to remember birthdays, anniversaries, or other card-sending occasions:

■ Write all the key dates for special occasions in your calendar at the beginning of the year (a good project for a cold January day). Then check the calendar the first of each month.

■ Purchase all the greeting cards you need for each month at one time. Then address and place stamps on them all at once so they are ready to be sent when you check your calendar. You can indicate the date to be sent in pencil next to the stamp. It will be covered by the postal mark once it goes through the mail.

■ Buy cards whenever you see any that might be appropriate for friends and family. Stack them in your desk drawer so you have them on hand.

■ Buy boxed assortments of all-occasion cards when you see them on sale.

■ Stock up on blank cards. Then you can write a personalized note no matter what the occasion.

■ Buy postcards and keep them in your purse, so when you are waiting in a doctor's office or at the beauty shop, you can write a brief note or hello to a far-away friend.

■ Keep disposable or instant cameras in the drawer with your thank-you notes. When you receive a beautiful bouquet of flowers, take a picture of yourself with the gift and include it in your thank-you note. The person who sent it will be able to see what they sent—and you, too! I do this all the time; it makes a lovely and memorable thank-you.

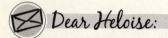 Dear Heloise:

When I open my Christmas cards, I save all of the envelopes, making sure each has the address on it. Then, when Christmas is over, I address my Christmas card envelopes for next year using this year's envelopes to go by. It takes just a few minutes to make changes or add new ones.

Personal Affairs Checklist

In case of an emergency, make sure you and your family know where the following are located:

- ☐ Phone numbers and addresses of all family members

- ☐ Family records (births, marriage, divorce, Social Security numbers, military service, citizenship)

- ☐ Bank account (number, locations)

- ☐ Safe-deposit box (key and location, person authorized to open it)

- ☐ Credit card numbers and charge accounts

- ☐ Doctor and hospital information

- ☐ Insurance policy information with the company name and where policy is kept (phone numbers, agents, beneficiaries)

- ☐ Financial/legal advisers (names and phone numbers)

- ☐ Debts (your own and owed to you)

- [ ] Pension plans, IRAs, Keoghs

- [ ] Brokerage accounts (with brokers' name and phone numbers)

- [ ] Business records

- [ ] A copy of will and trust agreements

- [ ] Funeral information (preferences, location of cemetery plots, deeds, any prearranged paperwork)

Dear Heloise:

Videotape or take photos of your important possessions, valuable items, or jewelry. This is a proof of ownership and shows their condition. Include a description. Keep a matching list with the original cost or any other information that could help you make an insurance claim, if anything is lost in a fire or by theft.

Financial Records

It's essential to keep all your financial records in order. Prepare envelopes, set up file folders, or use computer software programs to keep track of receipts and payments in the money-use categories listed below. If you use a computer to organize your records, be sure to print out a copy or two of this information or keep it on disk in case your computer crashes or breaks down.

- Bank accounts (checking, savings, money-market accounts, certificates of deposit)

- Food

- Household expenses (supplies, maintenance)

- Mortgage or rent costs

- Retirement plans (IRAs, Keoghs, pension)

- Social Security

- Taxes (federal, state, property)

- Utility bills

- Stocks and bonds

- Transportation

- Travel

- Entertainment

- Miscellaneous

 *Classic Hint*

Put irreplaceable documents into a safe-deposit box, but keep copies of these records in a home safe or in a plastic bag in the freezer.

A System for Bill Paying

When you pay bills on time, you can get lower interest rates and avoid those costly penalties for overdue payments. If you're constantly forgetting to pay bills, set up a paying system that works for you—either paying bills as soon as you get them or always on the first or fifteenth of the month, or online by setting up an automatic payment through your bank.

- Indicate bill due dates on a calendar.

- Note the due date under the envelope flap or where the stamp goes.

- Place a stamp and address label on the return envelope.

- Place in a folder, basket, or drawer by due date. Or organize bills in chronological order in a napkin holder, desk organizer, or close to the front door to be ready to be mailed.

- Print out labels with the company address to paste on envelopes, if necessary.

- Save postage costs by paying in person, if you can.

- Mail bills at least 5–7 days ahead of the due date to avoid late charges.

Here are my additional hints for keeping track of unpaid bills:

- Use a three-ring notebook (with pocket folders) to track bills. At the beginning of each month, put all bills and receipts into designated pockets—car insurance, household payments, utilities, etc. Write the check number on the bill it's written for. Note the interest paid, all income, and all payments on pocket folders. When tax time comes, you'll have all the information handy. After you pay your taxes, tie up the notebook and store it in a safe place.

- Keep a list of each unpaid bill, the due date, and the amount. Cross off each bill from the list as it gets paid. Then file the receipts, marked with check numbers, into folders designated for the specific categories, such as car, utilities, and house payments.

Maintaining Your Checkbook Register

Your check register is the best record of your deposits and spending, so always record your transactions. Include the date, check number, payee name, and invoice number. Balance your checkbook monthly.

- Attach a paper clip to the page in the check register you are filling up.

- Write in dark ink rather than pencil; it's easier to read.

- Use red ink in the register for tax-deductible payments, or mark such payments with a "T."

- Keep a small calculator in or near your register.

- Track monthly expenses at the back of the checkbook.

- Keep an extra register to keep track of all credit card spending. You won't be surprised at the amount when your credit card statement comes.

- When making one of a series of payments on an account, note on the register exactly what number payment it is.

- Write the exact period covered by the check payment for utilities, club dues, or magazine subscriptions.

- Always indicate on the check who or what it's for, particularly if you don't deal regularly with the company or person.

- Carry a spare check or two in your wallet or purse.

Credit Cards

■ Take all your credit cards and place them on a photocopier. Make several copies, and place one in your bank safe-deposit box and keep another at home in a safe place. If cards are stolen or lost, you will have a record of the numbers close at hand. You won't panic because you don't know the numbers!

■ Store credit cards and your passport in one designated place. A woman I know put her passport into a book in a book-case. When she looked for it, she could not remember which book! She never found it and had to get a new passport.

■ Enter the phone number of billing companies into your check register or onto a list so they will be easily available if you have to call about a payment problem or other emergency.

Tax Filing

As you prepare your taxes, having the right forms and personal files on hand is very important. Use this checklist:

☐ Appropriate tax forms, such as 1040 and 1099 forms (dividend and interest income)

☐ W-2 forms

☐ Canceled checks and checkbook registers

☐ Receipts for charitable contributions

☐ Deductible expenses receipts

☐ Property-tax receipts

☐ Records of mortgage interest paid

☐ Brokerage confirmations

For those who are self-employed, set up a bookkeeping system that records expenses and lists receipts according to tax-deduction categories (income, repairs, travel, dues and publications, meals, entertainment, etc.).

Check with your accountant or tax preparer before you throw out personal files, but follow these general guidelines:

- Utility, telephone, and water company statements and canceled checks should be kept for six months to a year (unless you want to keep them to compare costs from year to year). Always save checks used for home improvements, big-ticket items, or any deductible costs.

- Check with your financial institution about guidelines for retaining bank statements and canceled checks.

- Save all paperwork on investments and major purchases.

- Always keep copies of tax returns, receipts, canceled checks, and important tax records. Bundle each year and store in well-marked boxes.

- Visit www.irs.gov for information about how long to keep tax forms.

9

Entertaining

For many people, entertaining and hosting holiday parties can be highly stressful. There seems to be such high expectations for the perfect dinner party or family gathering. I say, a pox on that! The point is to have friends and family all together for a fun time.

My dear friend Merry never worries about entertaining. Her family always had big dinner parties as she was growing up. She can put together an impromptu party for forty in about two hours! However, for most of us, I think the key to making these events happen with the least stress is advance planning—that means making lists! The more organized you are, the more smoothly your event or party will go.

My husband, David, a fabulous cook, loves to barbecue everything! After years of throwing our casual Texas parties, I have three simple guidelines to make occasions less stressful for me as host and for my guests:

1. *Plan in advance.* Whether you are barbecuing on the patio or having the entire family over for a holiday meal, give your party some thought—as far ahead of the date as you can. When you have the date and occasion in mind, start making lists of attendees, a menu, and items you will need to have on hand.

2. *Make it simple.* Don't try a complicated menu or new dishes. Focus on what you do best and think about how you can make it easier—from using paper products to partially prepared foods. Everyone is busy, and in my opinion, there's no shame in taking shortcuts to make your dinner party easier.

3. *Accept help.* Swallow your pride. If a guest wants to bring something, tell him or her exactly what you'd like. Check your list to see what you least would like to do and let your guest bring that item. One reader writes that she's fussy about preparing all the food but always lets her guests bring wine.

During the party, if anyone offers to help, take them up on it. They can refill ice coolers or pass appetizers. However, although many people will offer to help clean up (clear off the dishes or even do kitchen duty), in this case, I think guests should be guests— and not just because it's the polite thing to do. A friend once relented and let her guests remove dishes and take them to the kitchen. One of her best friends accidentally dropped one of her favorite plates, one that could not be replaced. She wasn't angry, but she now declines any help after the meal. If you have heirloom china or valuable crystal, you should handle it yourself.

You set the rules for what's important to you in making your gathering a success. For me, it's planning in advance and doing as much as possible before the day of the party. Hello, freezer!

Dear Heloise:

I have an easy way to make entertainment simple and fun. It's all done with a big S-M-I-L-E.

S: Set the table early.

M: Menu. Select a good one! Try make-it-now, bake-it-later dishes.

I: Invite a mixture of interesting people and welcome a newcomer to your regular crowd.

L: Lists. Write it all down. Plan your schedule ahead of time, post it in a place for all to see, and if you stick to it, all will go as planned.

E: Enjoy, enjoy, enjoy. Entertaining can be loads of fun if you are at peace.

Organizing a Party

Classic Hint

My mother had a great hint for handling holiday parties. Instead of giving one huge party, she had small parties on two consecutive nights. She figured that she already cleaned the house, bought the flowers, and had plenty of food on hand. As she said, "Sure you may be tired after giving two parties in a row, but I'll bet you'll thank yourself for trying it this way when you realize how much time, energy, and money you saved."

Whether you host casual or more formal gatherings, making lists will help you put together and keep track of all the details.

Here's an easy way to plan any party:

1. *Who* is coming? Make your guest list and count the number of people.

2. *What* kind of party will you have? Will it be a formal sit-down bash, patio barbecue, or pot-luck gathering? Will you be serving brunch, lunch, dinner, or cocktails—with a lot or a few hors d'oeuvres?

3. *When* will you be hosting this event? Select a date and time.

4. *Where* are you having this party? If it's at home, make sure you have enough room to accommodate your guests. If it's elsewhere, you'll have to make arrangements well in advance.

5. *How* will you invite guests? If it's a casual or impromptu party, you can just call your guests. For other parties, purchase or make invitations and send them as soon as you can—no later than two weeks before the party. Generally, the more formal the gathering, the farther in advance you should send invitations.

You can save money on invitations by creating them on your computer. Double-check the invitation to be sure you've included the following information: who is hosting, the kind of party, the occasion, the date and time, the address and directions, and how to dress. Don't forget to include your phone number! Ask your guests to RSVP so you can plan for the amount of food and drink you will need to have. Formal events and wedding invitations should include acceptance cards with a stamped envelope.

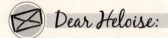 *Dear Heloise:*

I always include a small map of how to get to our house, along with our phone number, in the invitation. That way no one will have difficulty finding the house. I also tie ribbons or balloons on the tree and mailbox in our front yard.

Menu Planning

In my book, the easiest way to plan a meal is simply to make another list. Create a complete list of everything you're going to serve. Make a time line, too, so you'll know when to prepare, assemble, and cook (include times and temperatures).

Heloise's Party Shopping List

Write down the ingredients and supplies you'll need if you plan to make any dishes in these categories:

Hors d'oeuvres

Hot hors d'oeuvres
Cold hors d'oeuvres
Crudites or dip
Bread
Butter, margarine

Toppings, such as garlic or
   olive oil
Serving basket, bread board,
   spreaders, or dishes
Serving dishes and utensils

Entrées

Meat/fish
Casseroles
Sauces

Garnishes
Serving dishes and utensils

Side Dishes
Starch
Vegetable(s)

Salad
Serving dishes and utensils

Desserts
Cakes or pies
Garnishes, such as whipped
    cream or cream, fruits,
    mint leaves, or chocolate
    shavings

Serving plates, bowls,
    utensils, and extra napkins

Cheeses
Crackers
Crisp breads
Garnishes like grapes or
    parsley

Cheese board or plate,
    spreaders, knife,
    toothpicks for cubes
Small dessert plates

Nuts
Serving dishes
Small spoon for scooping

Small napkins

Mints or Chocolates
Serving dish, bowl, plate

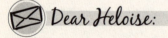 Dear Heloise:

When I plan to serve a rather elegant, complicated meal, I usually
choose a recipe I can make a day ahead or a recipe for my slow
cooker or microwave. I spread the work evenly over the day so my

family is not inconvenienced, my kitchen is not full of last-minute dirty dishes, and best of all, I'm calm, rested, and able to participate fully in the festivities.

Beverages

Event-planning experts estimate that people have about two or three drinks during the first two hours of a party and fewer later. A party is a good excuse to stock your bar, then you will have beverages available for last-minute or future parties.

You can figure out how much to buy simply by multiplying numbers of guests times two or three drinks. Of course, the amount of drinks consumed can vary also by the kind and length of party and the time of day. But it's probably best to buy more than you will think you will need. You don't want to run out—of anything! The following information will help you figure out beverage quantities for your party.

Hard Liquor and Wine

When serving, use a jigger to measure drinks. Here's roughly what you can get from various bottles of liquor:

1 liter hard liquor (33.8 ounces) = 22 (1 1/2-ounce) drinks.
1 bottle wine (liter size) = 10 (3-ounce) servings.
750 mL dessert wine = 10 (2 1/2-ounce) servings.
1 bottle champagne (1 quart) = 5 glasses, while a magnum
    will offer 10 glasses, and a jeroboam 21 glasses.
1 gallon punch = 40 punch-cup servings.

Of course, the size of your serving glasses will affect the amount, too. Plan on two drinks per person or more depending on your crowd.

If you are going to drink wines in the future, don't store the bottles upright. Corked wines should be placed on their sides. Before the party, store wines in a cool, dark place, such as the cellar. Whites and roses should be chilled, while red wines usually are served at room temperature.

To cool wine fast (in about 20 to 30 minutes), put it into an ice bucket with two-thirds crushed ice and one-third water. In the refrigerator, it will take about 1 1/2 to 2 1/2 hours to chill it to 40 or 45 degrees.

For champagne, you may just open a bottle for a first drink or a toast, so you don't have to buy a huge quantity, except for a wedding. Store champagne on its side in a cool, dark spot. Put it into the refrigerator or bucket of ice water about two hours before serving.

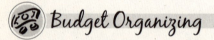 Budget Organizing

- If you need buckets to hold wine, beer, or soft drinks, use large plastic bowls, plastic baby bathtubs, wading pools, and kitchen or bar sinks. Just select something that will not leak. One reader admitted that she put bath towels in the clothes washer and then added the canned drinks and ice. I know other people who use their bathtubs as coolers. Clean it out well first!

- Big ice cubes needed to chill a punch can be made in clean margarine tubs or other containers that can be put into the freezer. Add fruit slices, strawberries, grapes, or maraschino cherries before freezing to provide color and interest to the punch bowl.

Bar Basics

Bourbon	Red and white wine
Blended whiskey	Beers: regular, light, and
Canadian whiskey	nonalcoholic
Gin	Port wine
Rum	Cream sherry
Scotch	After-dinner liqueurs
Vodka	

Mixers

Bitter lemon	Tomato and fruit juices
Club soda	Tonic water
Ginger ale	Soft drinks, diet and regular
Mineral water	

Serving and Decorating

Be creative when setting up the decorations and serving items for your party. Remember that not everything has to be used for its original purpose.

I have a friend who often has large, buffet-style parties. She lines narrow wicker baskets, then she places knives in one, forks in another, and spoons in the third. Look around your house and see what objects you have that could be used in another way for your party. Pull out all those unused ashtrays, wash well, and fill them with mints or candies. Those once-popular bonbon dishes could be used to hold grated cheese or jelly.

■ Have an old punch bowl sitting around? Use it to serve a large salad.

- A long wooden French bread holder is a perfect server for silverware.

- Cool cut-up veggies in an ice bucket. It's also great for serving them at a picnic.

- For casual events, use washcloths as napkins and terry-cloth towels as place mats.

- Pick greenery from your backyard to use in a centerpiece. Pinecones, wild flowers, and ivy can be used and then add fruit or flowers or peppers to complete an arrangement.

- To have a keepsake of a memorable party, lay a solid-color tablecloth or sheet over the table (use a pad underneath). Provide felt-tips or fabric pens to have every guest autograph the cloth or write a comment or poem.

- If you have a sit-down dinner, make place cards to indicate where people should sit. One cute idea is to use an instant camera to take a photo of each guest as they arrive, and then use the photos as place cards.

Servingware Checklist

If you are using china, check to make certain you've got what you need for the bash. For picnics and barbecues, see if you have enough paper and plastic servingware on hand. Get your serving supplies organized in advance:

☐ Plates: hors d'oeuvres, dinner, salad, bread and butter, dessert

☐ Bowls: soups, flat pasta, dessert

☐ Bowls, platters, and compotes for serving courses

☐ Flatware: knives, forks (dinner, salad, dessert), and spoons (soup, tea, or coffee)

☐ Cups or mugs for hot drinks

☐ Glasses: wine and cocktail glasses, punch cups, glasses or mugs for soft drinks and beer, and water glasses

☐ Serving utensils: large spoons, serving spatulas, relish spoons and forks, large meat fork, carving knives, salad servers, butter knives, cheese and spread servers, pie servers, and cake knives

☐ Warming trays, chafing dishes, and sterno packs

☐ Tablecloth(s), place mats, napkins, bread cloths, and doilies

☐ Centerpiece(s)

☐ Trivets to protect the table

☐ Water or juice pitchers and coffee and tea servers

Party Safety

Set out these things the day of the party, just in case there's an emergency:

■ Place a fire extinguisher in your kitchen and another in the party area.

■ If you are using candles, place a bottle of water in the same room, just in case they tip over.

■ If you are barbecuing, bring a large jug of water and a box of baking soda to keep near the fire.

- For an outdoor gathering, keep bug repellent on hand and salve to soothe bites.

- Keep an emergency guide that shows how to perform the Heimlich maneuver, in case anyone chokes, and cardiopulmonary resuscitation (CPR), should they stop breathing.

- Finally, be sure to check out the electrical outlets where you will plug in warming trays, chafing dishes, or coffeemakers. You don't want to have cords dangling in the traffic flow. Also, too many appliances plugged into one circuit can blow fuses.

Big Party Planning

If you are hosting a really big party for a wedding, family reunion, or other special event, planning several months in advance is essential. Many of these require a larger space than your home, so you may need to find outside space. When you have decided on the size of the party and have made the guest list, then the real planning begins. You will need to:

- Choose a restaurant or hall and book it as far in advance as you can.

- Buy or print invitations and mail them at least four to six weeks in advance of the event.

- Hire a caterer (see "Booking a Caterer," p. 119).

- Make arrangements for renting tables, chairs, or other equipment.

- Select entertainment or music.

Booking a Caterer

For a big event, you need to find a reputable caterer and book their services up to a year in advance. Get references from friends who have used one and been happy with the food and service. Then call and meet with the caterer and ask for a sampling of the food you may want for your event.

- Take extensive notes on the specifics of food and beverage, how they will be presented and served, and what the serving schedule will be.

- Establish the per-person price. Will dessert, wine, and/or open bar be included?

- Set a date for you to give the final head count and determine the cut-off date for last-minute guests. Find out if you will be billed for no-shows. Generally, that is the case.

- Get exact fees for bartending and wait staff.

- Ask about who provides any tableware, serving utensils, trays, table linens, and centerpieces. If this is a more casual affair, who buys the disposable plates, cups, and napkins?

- How much cleanup does the caterer do, and what will happen to the leftovers?

- Once you have agreed on all the details, get a written contract, which covers everything decided on, and sign it.

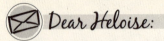 *Dear Heloise:*

When our daughter married several years ago, we were in temporary housing.

This caused a serious shortage of space to keep things I gathered for the occasions. I finally had a brainstorm and began collecting large shopping bags, which I labeled *church, rehearsal dinner, bridal brunch, showers,* etc. This is a perfect way to keep all the things together and not have to hunt for them.

Dear Reader: You can also recycle other containers, like tote bags or sturdy cardboard boxes, for party organizing.

Keep Parties on File!

Many party-givers I know have extensive files and recipe boxes filled with ideas for family gatherings and specific seasonal parties. Other readers keep records of what they served at each party and who were the guests, so they never repeat the same meal. For dinner guests you'll be having again, write down allergies to foods and vegetarian or health restrictions such as no-salt.

Many readers have written to me about how they store all recipes, party plans, and shopping lists in their computers and print out the information when they need it. Here are some of my favorite ways:

■ Create a family master list that includes all names, phone numbers, addresses, and e-mail addresses to make it faster to contact people for parties.

- Organize recipes by month, season, occasion, or alphabetically.

- Place napkins, paper plates, linens, and/or accompanying decorations in a plastic box or bin with recipes. Label the boxes clearly, and store them in the attic, basement, or garage.

Dear Heloise:

Keep a file in a large zipper-locking plastic bag for each holiday (Valentine's Day, Easter, Christmas, etc.). In each bag, you can put leftover cards, party napkins, gift wrap, stickers, decorations, and even paper party plates. Just a glance in the bag will show what you need to buy to supplement the leftovers when the holiday rolls around again.

Dear Reader: A large see-through plastic bin can do the job, too!

PART THREE

Organized and on the Go

10

Shopping

The average American family of four spends thousands of dollars a year on groceries. If you think you spend too much money, take some time to examine the way you shop. Do you feel like you're always at the store, making trips three or four times a week? Do you roam up and down the aisles, putting into your cart whatever food catches your eye? Is your purse so messy you have trouble finding your wallet—let alone coupons? Organizing your shopping trips can save you time at the store and cash in your budget.

These are my five strategies for efficient shopping:

- *Make menus in advance.* Plan your upcoming week's meals—every one of them.

- *Write a grocery list*—it's one of the best tools you have for saving time and money.

- *Clip coupons.* Compare your menus and grocery lists with

coupons you have been saving, and use them to save on your grocery bills.

■ *Take advantage of supermarket specials.* Look for supermarket ads in your local newspaper. They often have weekly sales. Match your shopping needs with these offers.

■ *Shop only once a week.* Infrequent trips to the store eliminate short but time- and gas-consuming treks and discourage expensive impulse buying.

Start in Your Kitchen

The best place to start shopping is in your kitchen. Take an inventory of what you have in the cupboards and in the refrigerator. If you already have your food well organized (see Chapter 2, "The Kitchen"), then this won't be so hard. As you plan your menus for the week and write your shopping list, you should know what you have on hand (especially dated items) and what you'll need to buy.

Create a Shopping List

If you write down each dinner you prepare for a month on separate index cards, creating your grocery list becomes a simple matter of pulling out enough index cards for the number of meals you'll be shopping for. Your food shopping list is always ready-made! Plus, thanks to all the food websites online, you will never run out of menus, recipes, or meal ideas.

If you have a computer at home, you can save all sorts of menu and recipe files that can be called up and printed out whenever you're ready to shop or cook. It also saves time to keep a master shopping list, which will remind you to check for those things you usually forget. You can keep track of what you buy and then revise your list and run off a supply of lists every three months or so.

- Plan weekly meals by taking into consideration the leftovers you have and by finding out what's on sale. See what you have on hand and then add needed ingredients to your list. If you are trying new recipes, double-check to make sure you have all the ingredients.

- To save recipes cut from magazines or printed from websites, tape them to index cards and file them in plastic recipe boxes or even shoe boxes.

- Store recipes alphabetically in an inexpensive binder with sheet protectors, file folders, or a binder-style photo album.

- Make a preprinted shopping list. Organize your list by types of items, or follow the layout of your supermarket. (For a sample list, see page 128.)

- If you shop at the same store or two, organize your grocery list by the order in which you find things in the aisles, or set up the list by category—produce, paper goods, etc. Try not to waste time doubling back for things in the same aisle.

- Clip your shopping list and any coupons to be used onto a small clipboard before going to the store. The board also provides a firm backing so you can check off the items on your list as you put them in your cart. Attach a piece or two of blank paper under the list for quick computing or noting prices for future reference.

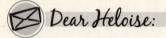
Dear Heloise:

I keep a sticky pad of notepaper on my refrigerator door. When I run out of any item, I write it on the pad and lift off the sheet before a shopping trip. At the store, I stick the sheet to the handle of the grocery cart for easy access.

Heloise's Master Shopping List

Breads, Cereals, and Pasta

Breads
- Sliced
- Specialty
- Rolls

Cereals
- Dry
- To cook

Chips, tortillas, snacks
Crackers
Other
Pasta
Rice
- White
- Brown

Fresh Fruits

Apples
Bananas
Cherries
Grapefruit
Grapes
Lemons
Limes

Melons
Oranges
Peaches
Pears
Plums
Other

Fresh Vegetables

Artichokes
Asparagus
Avocado

Broccoli
Carrots
Cauliflower

Celery

Corn

Corn on the cob

Cucumbers

Green beans

Green onions

Lettuce

Mushrooms

Onions

Peas

Peppers

Potatoes

Sprouts

Squash

Sweet potatoes

Tomatoes

Zucchini

Other

Frozen Foods

Artichokes

Asparagus

Breakfast foods

Broccoli

Carrots

Cauliflower

Corn

Corn on the cob

Dinners

French fries

Fruit

Green beans

Ice cream

Juices

Mixed vegetables

Pastry

Peas

Pizza

Other

Dairy Case

Butter

Cheese

- Cottage
- Cream
- Grated/shredded
- Sliced

Eggs

Margarine

Milk

- 1%
- 2%
- Buttermilk
- Cream
- Whole

Yogurt

Other

Meat Counter

Bacon	Sausage
Beef	Seafood
Chicken	Turkey
Luncheon meat	Other
Pork	

Sweets

Cake	Sweet rolls
Cookies	Other

Groceries

Canned fruit	Shortening
Canned meat	Soups
Canned tuna	Tomato products
Canned vegetables	Vinegar
Cooking/salad oils	Other canned goods
Nonstick spray	

Beverages

Beer	Tea
Bottled water	Soda
Coffee	Wine
Juices	

Herbs, Spices, and Baking Supplies

Baking powder
Baking soda
Condiments
- Bottled sauces

- Catsup
- Mayo
- Mustard
- Olives

- Pickles
- Salad dressings
- Other
Cornmeal
Flour
- All-purpose
- Bread
- Whole-wheat
- Other
Gelatin
Jams and jellies

Peanut butter
Spices
- Pepper
- Salt
- Other
Sugar
- Brown
- Confectioners'
- Substitutes
- White
- Other

General Merchandise
Cosmetics
Deodorant
Dishwasher detergent
Fabric softener/sheets
Laundry detergent
Liquid dish detergent

Pet food
Shampoo
Soap
Toothpaste
Vitamins
Other cleaning supplies

Miscellaneous

_____   _____

_____   _____

_____   _____

✉ *Dear Heloise:*

My mother came up with this idea for people who shop for others.
She'd write her grocery list and then put the front labels from the

products in an envelope. That way she knew the exact size, brand, and weight she wanted to purchase.

Dear Reader: I do the same, just as my mother taught me to do. This also helps if family members will tear off the labels and put them with the shopping list.

Coupons

Take pride in being able to stay within your budget. Instead of looking at careful shopping as a chore, view it as a game. I have a friend who likes to see if she can save 10 percent of the total bill when she uses coupons to shop for staples. Coupons are a great way to save money, but only if you use them to get discounts on items you will actually use.

You can buy specially designed coupon organizers, but I like to store coupons in envelopes, which I keep in the kitchen near my shopping lists. I file my coupons by food category and put those with the earliest expiration date at the front. I also write a "C" next to any item on the shopping list that has a corresponding coupon in the envelope.

Budget Organizing

Make your own coupon organizer from an old checkbook cover, with the to-be-used coupons in one side pocket and coupons for your shopping trip in the other pocket.

■ Place coupons in an envelope in the order of the supermarket aisles, and write a list on the outside.

- Save envelopes from junk mail to store coupons.

- Use a highlighter to mark the expiration date on coupons.

- File coupons according to expiration date.

- Toss out coupons for items you normally don't purchase.

- Shop at stores that offer double coupons.

- Trade coupons with family, friends, and co-workers.

- Purchase several newspapers or magazines to get extra coupons. The Sunday paper is usually crammed with coupons.

Dear Heloise:

I made a coupon organizer by cutting out pictures of food categories—meats, dairy, etc.—from grocery fliers. I stuck the pictures on individual envelopes and put each coupon in the appropriate one. Then, I put all the envelopes together in a single clutch-style envelope. Now it's easy to pull out the required coupon when I'm in a hurry.

Organize Your Purse

From credit cards to cosmetics, from family photos to house keys, a woman's daily life is in her purse. We look through our handbags a dozen times a day, yet how much time do we spend hunting for the items we need? So before you toss your grocery list inside, take a few minutes to organize your bag.

The easiest way to clean out your purse is to use the A-B-C method of organizing. Empty out the contents of your day purse or several handbags if you tend to use more than one regularly. Divide the contents into three piles: essential items, such as car keys, wallet, and checkbook (A); optional items, like notepads and cosmetics (B), and obvious trash, like candy wrappers (C). Throw away group C. Among the items in group B, any items you haven't used on the go in the past week should be removed. Find an appropriate home for them in your house, or toss them.

Put A items back in your purse. Place your wallet and keys inside a zippered pocket, if the bag has one. Separate cosmetics, coupons, pens, etc. into groups, and put each group into small resealable plastic bags. It's easier to sort through a few plastic bags than myriad individual items.

- Carry a mid-size day purse. Too small and you'll need an extra bag to hold important items; too big and it's easily filled with junk you don't really need to tote.

- The bigger the bag, the easier it is to "lose" an item in your purse.

- Try to put frequently used items, such as your wallet and keys, in the same spot every time so you will always know where they are.

- If you have lots of change at the bottom of your purse, consider carrying a change purse in addition to your wallet. Use up the change whenever you purchase small items.

- If your wallet is brimming with cards—credit cards, discount cards, business cards—remove all but the ones you use on a weekly basis. Put the rest in a spare wallet that you keep at home until needed. Cancel credit cards you haven't used in more than a year.

■ Clean out your purse on a weekly basis, tossing or filing cash receipts and discarding old shopping lists and gum wrappers!

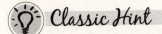 **Classic Hint**

Before a day of running errands, put a plastic laundry basket in the trunk of your car. After you shop, put the packages in the basket. Small bags don't get lost, and you can carry in the basket with all the bags in one trip when you get home.

When You Get to the Supermarket

You'll save on your grocery bill by cutting back on impulse shopping. Remember that stores are designed to promote impulse buying. The most expensive items are placed on shelves that are at eye level; the idea is to get you to grab the first thing you see. Try to limit your grocery shopping trips to once a week. It used to be that people shopped daily for fresh goods, but nowadays the reality is, the more trips you make to the supermarket, the more impulse buys you will make.

■ Go to the supermarket early in the morning or during major sports events or popular TV shows when it is less crowded.

■ Eat before you shop, or you'll be tempted to buy just about anything that looks good!

■ Have a complete shopping list handy and check off items as you get them.

- Buy your most-used items in bulk when they are on sale.

- Buy items to prepare. Pre-packed and pre-cooked meals cost more.

✉ *Dear Heloise:*

Whenever I'm going to the grocery store, I take along a cooler with one or more ice packs inside. I ask for all the frozen items to be bagged separately. When putting the bagged groceries into the car, I place all the frozen items into the cooler. This works well especially for ice cream in the summer.

Dear Reader: You also won't have to pass up a good buy on milk or meat. Then you don't have to worry if you need to make extra stops en route home. And if anything spills, it will be contained and much easier to clean up!

When Products Go on Sale

Knowing when to shop for all kinds of sale items can save you money. Follow this yearly calendar for best buys:

After-Christmas sales—Jan.

Air conditioners—Feb.,
   July, Aug.

Appliances—Jan., Mar.,
   Oct., Nov.

Appliances (small)—Sept.

Art supplies—Jan., Feb.

Auto accessories—May

Baby carriages—Jan.

Back-to-school specials—
   Aug.

Bathing suits—July, Aug.

Bedding—Feb., June

Bicycles—Feb., Sept.

Blankets and quilts—May, Nov., Dec.

Books—Jan.

Boots—Feb.

Boys' and girls' shoes —Mar.

Boys' clothing—June

Boys' suits and coats—Nov.

Building supplies—June

Camping equipment—Aug.

Car parts (batteries/mufflers) —Sept.

Carpets and rugs—Jan., Aug.

Cars (new)—Sept.

Cars (used)—Feb., Oct., Dec.

Children's clothes—July, Dec.

China—Jan., Mar., Sept., Oct.

Christmas promotions— Dec.

Clocks—Sept.

Clothing—Mar.

Coats and hats—Oct., Nov., Dec.

Cosmetics—Aug.

Costume jewelry—Jan.

Curtains and drapes—Feb., Aug.

Diamond jewelry—Jan.

Electronic equipment—July

Fabrics—Apr., June, Sept., Nov.

Fans—Aug.

Fishing equipment—Oct.

Floor coverings—June

Furniture—Jan., Feb., Mar., July, Aug., Sept., Nov.

Furs—Jan., Aug.

Garden supplies—Mar.

Gardening equipment—July, Aug., Sept.

Glassware—Jan., Mar., Sept.

Gloves—Feb.

Handbags—May, July

Hardware—Sept.

Hosiery—Apr.

Housewares—May, Oct.

Ice skates—Mar.

Jewelry—May

Lingerie—Jan., Apr., Nov.

Liquor—Dec.

Luggage—Jan., Mar., May, Oct.

Men's apparel—Feb.

Original art—July

Outdoor furniture—May

Painting supplies—Apr.

Radios—Jan., Feb., July

Ranges—Apr.

Resort and cruisewear—Dec.

Rugs—May, July

School supplies—Aug., Oct.

Shoes—Jan., Dec.

Silver/silverware—Oct.

Ski equipment—Mar.

Sportswear and equipment—
Feb., July

Stereos—Apr., Oct.

Suits—Dec.

Suits/dresses (post Easter)—
Apr.

Summer clothes—June

Tires—May

Toys—Jan., Feb., Dec.

TVs—Jan., Feb., May, June,
July, Oct.

Water heaters—Jan.

White sales—Jan., May.,
Aug., Nov.

Wine—Apr.

Winter clothing—Nov.

Winter sports equipment—
Jan., July

Women's coats—Aug., Oct.

Women's shoes—Apr.

(© Heloise, Inc., 2004)

11

Travel and Vacations

Vacations are supposed to be relaxing getaways, but how many of these trips just make us more stressed? I've received many letters from readers about travels gone awry, when many hassles—from lost luggage to double-booked hotel rooms—might have been prevented with simple precautions. Where should you go, what should you take, what should you do when you arrive, and how should you leave your home behind? Of course, you can't prepare for everything (least of all the weather!), but a little bit of advance planning can go a long way toward making your vacation what it was meant to be—a vacation.

Planning a Trip

Your family, like mine, probably has a favorite vacation spot, whether it's the beach, the mountains, or someplace even more exotic! No matter your destination, planning ahead is key to having a good time and saving money.

Hotels, airlines, car rentals, and travel packages often require advance booking, and usually making a reservation is a good idea anyway. Often, the longer in advance you book, the cheaper the fare, cruise, or room. If you travel in a region's off-season, rates may also be cheaper.

You can make reservations through a travel agent or by yourself online. If you use an agent, you have the benefit of discussing the types of trips you enjoy and learning about your travel options without having to do much of the legwork yourself. But it is easy today to book air tickets, hotel reservations, and just about everything else you need for a trip on the Internet or by calling 800 numbers. There are a number of established reservation websites you can rely on. In addition, almost all airlines, hotels, and popular travel destinations have websites.

- Determine what your travel budget is.

- Specify your preferred travel dates and times. Have a backup schedule ready.

- Share any medical requirements, physical disabilities, special diets, and smoking or nonsmoking needs.

- Identify your frequent traveler or flyer number or programs.

Purchasing Airline Tickets

- Consider what's more important to you—the cost or the flight schedule. Can you fly at a less convenient time to save money?

- Determine if you are able to change the reservations without a penalty.

- If you will be flying around a popular holiday, such as Thanksgiving, make reservations several months in advance.

- Call to confirm a domestic flight a day or so before you are scheduled to leave. Confirm international flights at least 72 hours before flight time.

Know these terms before you book:

- *Add-on fare.* This is the cost of air travel to the city from which the tour is leaving.

- *All-inclusive.* This tour package price will include land arrangements along with round-trip airfare.

- *Force majeure.* These are activities or events that cannot be controlled or anticipated by a tour operator, such as a flood, fire, or act of terrorism.

- *Fly-drive tour.* This is an independent tour that also includes a rental car as part of the fee.

Do You Need Travel Insurance?

Before you talk with a travel agent about travel insurance, call your insurance agent to review your policies and determine if you will need any extra coverage.

A basic travel insurance policy may cover baggage loss, emergency evacuation, worldwide telephone assistance, accidents, sickness, and trip cancellation or interruption. There are policy limits on baggage and contents—make sure you read the fine print!

- If you are traveling to a single country or destination, you may not need extra insurance. However, if it's a long trip to a number of locations, or if you have special medical conditions, those could warrant more insurance.

- Check your health and homeowner's policies first to find out what they cover while you travel (baggage loss, health problems, theft, etc.).

- Be aware that if you cancel your trip because you change your mind, trip cancellation insurance may reimburse you for first-class tickets, but might not reimburse you for non-refundable discount tickets. Find out all the specifics before you buy this insurance.

Travel Documents

- When you have all your arrangements completed, make copies of airline tickets, rail passes, hotel reservations, credit cards, and passport numbers. Keep one copy at home or give it to a friend. Carry another copy in a resealable plastic bag in a carry-on or purse separate from the original documents—but these copies should not be left in luggage to be checked or that is otherwise out of your possession.

- Don't forget to call ahead to reconfirm hotel and airline reservations at least 24 to 48 hours prior to travel.

- If you are driving, pack your auto club membership card and then write down the phone numbers of certified towing services near the routes you will be taking that are sanctioned by your card.

- Bring along a card or sheet of paper with your names and all relevant information, such as whom to contact in case of emergency (at home and at your destination), the name of your medical insurance company, and the number of the policy.

- Keep another information card in your purse that contains the name of your family doctor, blood types of all family members, and any special medicines or allergies. Bring along a copy of prescriptions, and carry these drugs in their original containers.

- Check with your bank to see if there are ATMs in the areas where you are going to travel. Can you use your card to get cash? Will your bank charge you extra fees to do so?

- Get traveler's checks so you don't have to carry lots of cash. If traveler's checks are stolen, you can get reimbursed for them.

- Divide up credit cards between travelers. If a wallet or purse is lost or stolen, the other person will have cards to use.

In Heloise's Handbag

Wallet
- ATM card
- Cash
- Credit Cards
- Discount cards

- Driver's license
- Insurance card
- Traveler's checks

Passport (for international travel)

Airline/train tickets
Checkbook or just a few
  checks
Keys
- Car keys
- Hotel key
- House keys
- Rental car key

Flight information
- Airline name(s) and
  phone numbers
- Airport names
- Departure/arrival dates
  and times

- Flight numbers
- Reservation confirma-
  tionnumber

Hotel contact information
- Directions to hotel
- Hotel address and
  phone number
- Hotel name
- Reservation confirma-
  tion number

In case of emergency contact list
Packing list

How to Pack a Suitcase

If you write a list before you pack, you won't forget a thing. Just think of what you need from toe to top, and add to the list as items occur to you. Type it up on your computer and print out two copies, one for your purse (or carry-on) and one for the suitcase. Your children's packing list may include their favorite games, toys, etc. If you will be traveling to multiple destinations, check the list during the trip so you won't leave anything behind. Having a list also comes in handy if your luggage is stolen or lost.

When you travel by car, you can take as much luggage as will fit, but air travel is very limiting these days. Airlines usually charge extra for too many or too-heavy suitcases. Check with airlines to find out their maximum luggage weight for national flights.

Try to keep luggage to one suitcase and one carry-on bag per person. And when you're done making a list of the clothes each family member needs, look at the list and cross out half of it! Most people tend to overpack. Keep in mind that you can wear clothing several times in different combinations, especially if you're going on a casual vacation.

Here are my hints for making the most of your suitcase space:

- Pack heavy items in the bottom of the suitcase so they won't squash everything. (The bottom means whatever will be the bottom when the case is picked up.)

- Put shoes in sole-to-sole, with the heel of one shoe touching the toes of the other. Stuff small items, such as underwear and panty hose, into the shoes to save space and help shoes keep their shape.

- Roll your clothes to prevent wrinkled clothing. Lay each garment flat inside a plastic dry-cleaning bag and then roll up.

- Label your possessions. Put address stickers on cell phones, cameras, and your children's cherished toys. Place your home address and phone number or a business card inside your luggage tag—in case it's lost, they will be able to get it back to you.

- Pack toiletries in travel- or trial-size containers only.

- Be sure to monitor your children's packing and help them organize everything! (I have a friend whose child tried to pack her hamster in her bag!)

- Mark your luggage with a piece of brightly colored yarn or a sticker so it's easy to identify. This may also prevent another passenger from mistaking your bag as theirs. (For a rainy day project, have children paint flowers or a picture on their bags for easy identification.)

■ Instead of taking each piece of luggage into the motel every night, pack a separate plastic bag with just the things you will need for an overnight stop. Leave the rest in the car as long as it doesn't include irreplaceable or valuable items.

■ Pack an empty backpack. Use it to carry items needed or purchases during outings.

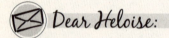 Dear Heloise:

It seems that I always overpack my suitcase when we visit my parents each summer. So when I returned home from the last trip, I made a list of everything I actually wore. This gave me a true idea of what I really need to pack. Next year I will be ready with my list, which I left inside my suitcase. I won't pack a bunch of clothes I won't wear!

In Heloise's Suitcase

Clothing	(#)		
Blouses	____	Shorts	____
Shirts	____	Suits	____
T-shirts	____	Pajamas	____
Sweaters	____	Underwear	____
Jeans	____	Scarf	____
Pants	____	Socks	____
Dresses	____	Shoes	____
Skirts	____	Swimwear	____

Toiletries (use travel-size containers)

Cosmetics	Razor and shaving cream
Toothbrush and toothpaste	Sunscreen
Soap	Facial tissues, packets of
Deodorant	wipes, cotton balls, swabs
Perfume	Bandages/adhesive pads
Lotion	

Miscellaneous

Sunglasses	Night-light
Extra pair of glasses/	Small flashlight
contact lenses	Ear plugs
Extra handbags	Sleep mask
Travel alarm clock	Plastic bags
Hair dryer	Photocopies of passport,
Sewing kit	driver's license, and
Children's toys, games,	airline tickets
and books	

Dear Heloise:

Instead of packing dry cotton pads and a bottle of astringent, I pre-moisten the amount of cotton balls I will need and pack them in a small, screw-top plastic container. The cotton helps hold the liquid, preventing messy and expensive spills of an entire bottle of toner in one's suitcase.

Dear Reader: Good idea. It's also wise to put anything that could leak in a sealable plastic bag—just in case.

Because I travel a great deal, I have also learned how to organize my carry-on suitcase for maximum efficiency. In fact, I keep a carry-on bag packed and ready to go at all times. I make a list of essentials I will need to keep with me in the car or on the plane, or in case of an emergency if I need to spend a night without my suitcase. In addition to reading material, I pack items such as medications, makeup, a change of clothing, business supplies, and breakable or valuable items.

In Heloise's Carry-On Bag

Book and/or magazines
Guidebook and maps
Itinerary
Travel headphones and CD, MP3, or cassette player
Cell phone, extra battery and charger
Camera and film
Small notebook, pen, and pencil
Address labels and stamps
Prescription medication (in original bottles)
Over-the-counter medication (headache, cold, stomach)
One change of clothing
Eyeglasses
Hairbrush
Tissues
Small makeup bag
Jewelry
Photocopies of passport, driver's license, and airline tickets
Packing list (contents of suitcase)

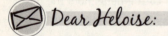 Dear Heloise:

When my children were young, I would pack their outfits in plastic zipper bags when traveling. Each bag would include shirt, shorts, socks, underpants, and even hair ribbons. They would just select a bag and be dressed. This eliminated the need for discussion about what to wear each day, and they didn't spend their last vacation days wearing clashing outfits.

Traveling by Car

If you and your family are taking a vacation a relatively short distance away, traveling by car rather than air can be an excellent way to save money. But make sure your car is up for the trip. Get your car tuned up, checked out (especially tires and belts), and serviced beforehand. Keep an emergency kit in the trunk (see below). And be sure to have your route well planned out, with maps and directions on hand. One major cause of vacation frustration is spending hours lost on unfamiliar roads.

Road Trip Emergency Kit

- ☐ Aerosol tire inflation products
- ☐ Auto club card
- ☐ Blanket
- ☐ Duct tape
- ☐ Flares
- ☐ Flashlights
- ☐ Gallon of water
- ☐ Gas can
- ☐ Jumper cables
- ☐ Matches
- ☐ Motor oil
- ☐ Road map
- ☐ Shovel
- ☐ Spare tire and jack
- ☐ Tool kit

"Are We There Yet?"

To make a long car trip pass happily without extensive whining, plan in advance. How are you going to keep your children busy, not bored, during the trip?

- Have each child pack one bag or backpack to keep in the car. They can fill it with their favorite items—CD players and headsets, electronic toys, books, games, crayons, etc.

- Keep bottled water and healthy snacks, along with wipes and paper towels, in the car.

- Store one bag filled with pillows, blankets, and clothing changes.

- Play scenery games with your children to see if they can find or count different state license plates, animals, vegetables, or people.

- Play "I Spy" and work your way through each letter of the alphabet. Have a treat for the winner.

- Bring videotapes or DVDs if you have a portable player that will work in your vehicle.

- Play audiobooks or CDs to help pass the time. You can rent these from many libraries. I have friends who drive from New York City to a country cottage every weekend. They play detective-story tapes, one side on the way and the other on the way back.

- Take rest stops every 2 hours or every 100 miles.

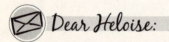 **Dear Heloise:**

To eliminate bulky suitcases on a car trip, I leave clothes on hangers, slip them inside a large plastic trash bag, and lay them flat in the trunk or on the backseat. When you travel with "plastic luggage" as I do, there's no need to unpack. On the return trip, the bags are used for soiled clothing.

Dear Reader: You can also use plastic bags instead of luggage to carry underwear, shoes, and toiletries.

Renting a Car

- Before you rent a car, check with your insurance agent to see if your rental car is covered by your policy. You won't need to add that pricey rental insurance. Did you know that some credit cards have coverage on rental cars if the fees are paid with that card? Ask in advance.

- Take time to figure out how to turn on the windshield wipers, headlights, air conditioner, heater, and radio before you leave the lot. Make certain there is an operating manual, spare tire, and jack, too. Do a walk around the vehicle before and after a trip. Make sure there are no dents or scratches!

- Get information on who to contact in the case of breakdown or accident before you leave the rental agency.

Renting an RV

Renting a recreational vehicle (RV) is more complicated, so put this information at the top of your to-do list.

- Compare information from local and national companies for seasonal rates. Determine which model would suit your travel/vacation needs. Generally, the longer you rent an RV, the bigger the discount.

- Find out if mileage is packaged to include the maximum number of miles. Ask about insurance, prep charges, or generator fees. You will pay for gas, so inquire about average fuel consumption.

- Double-check insurance coverage.

- Don't leave without getting contact numbers for emergencies.

- Call ahead to RV parks across the nation to get info on facilities and rates. Book ahead, too.

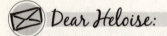 *Dear Heloise:*

My husband and I have a trailer and travel all around the country. When we are on a trip, I carry along a calendar and write on each date where we camped and the mileage we traveled that day. Having a calendar also helps when you take photographs and are unable to figure out where the picture was taken.

Traveling by Air

With all the changes in airport security today, getting to the airport early and staying organized is a must. Ask yourself, how can I make this trip a smoother, less-stressful experience? Designate what luggage each family member will carry. Make certain your children bring along their favorite items to help pass the time in case of delays.

- Ask for a bulkhead or exit row seat, where there is more legroom.

- Find out the luggage restrictions before you get to the airport! Know the sizes allowed for carry-ons. Check your children's bags, and pare down what you can before you leave the house.

- If you travel often, you might consider joining an airline club. These clubs offer special rooms at the airport where you and your family will be able to pass the time more comfortably.

Preventing Lost Luggage

- Remove old flight tags to avoid confusion. Check to make sure the correct tag is on the bag.

- Put an identification tag on the inside and outside of each bag.

- Avoid using obviously expensive luggage; it may attract thieves.

- Get to baggage claim as soon as possible to get your luggage.

- Keep your eyes on your luggage at all times. Never leave it unattended—not even for a moment.

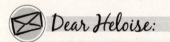 *Dear Heloise:*

To make it easier for the security people at airports to inspect the contents of the bag and to keep it from being a mess after inspection, a little organizing can speed up the process. Place like items in clear, plastic self-sealing bags that can be easily removed from

the suitcase. Emptied bags can also be used for dirty laundry on the trip home.

At the Hotel

There's nothing worse than arriving at a hotel after a long day of traveling, only to find that you're not a registered guest! To avoid confusion, always call ahead to confirm the reservation, the type of room, the number of nights, and the price. Ask for a confirmation number. Write down the exact name, address, and phone number of the hotel—sometimes there are several hotels with the same name in a city. This is especially important if you will be staying in different hotels during your trip.

- If there is a problem with your room, remain calm and ask to speak with the manager. Hotels want your business, and managers will usually do their best to solve a problem.

- If the room isn't what you expected, ask for an upgrade.

- If the hotel is full and your room has been given away, see if they can arrange for you to stay at another hotel.

- Plan your travel arrangements so you arrive around the designated check-in time, not after midnight.

- When you enter the hotel room, always put the hotel key in the same spot, like on top of the television or by the door. A hotel might charge you a fee if you lose the key.

- When you leave the hotel room for a day of sightseeing or for the beach, take stock of what you are carrying before you go. Count the number of items you have with you.

When you leave, count the items again. You'll know right away if an item is missing.

■ If you've made a checklist of what you have in your bag, be sure to check off items as you repack. It's too easy to leave behind an alarm clock or shoes under the bed. Give the room a final once-over before you check out.

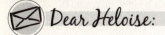 *Dear Heloise:*

When going on vacation, I put each family member's undergarments in a shoe box and stack them inside a suitcase. When I get to the hotel, I just lift out the boxes and put them in the dresser drawers. Everyone's clothes are organized and easy to find.

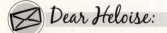 *Dear Heloise:*

We travel a lot by car and routinely stay in hotels. One of the chores I always hated was lugging in all the suitcases every night. So I came up with a solution. I now place each change of clothes in a plastic bag, and pack along with toiletry items in a small suitcase and I can just bring in that one.

Protecting Your Home While You're Away

Home safety experts say that when you leave for a trip, it's important to make sure your home does not look unattended.

■ Set timers that automatically turn on and off lights in several rooms at different times. Timers can also turn on and off radios.

- Park a vehicle halfway up the driveway so it blocks the garage door.

- Disconnect your automatic garage-door opener when you leave for a vacation. Someone else may have the same frequency and your garage door could be opened.

- Ask a neighbor to pick up your mail and newspapers, or have the post office and your delivery carrier hold them while you are gone.

- If you will be away for a long trip, hire a neighbor or teenager to mow or water your lawn or shovel the snow. There are professional house-sitting services that can do the job, too.

- Have a neighbor park their car in your driveway.

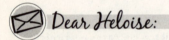 Dear Heloise:

Before going away for a trip, I turn the telephone ringer to low and the answering machine volume all the way down. No one outside will hear when the phone rings or messages are left—a sure sign I'm not home.

12

Moving

When the house-hunting is over, then the *real* planning begins! Organization is key in preparing the contents of your home for a move. Moving is an ideal time to clean out old stuff and get rid of things you no longer use. After all, it's expensive to move. You do not want to pay extra to haul your junk! So throw out all that ancient history and have a garage sale. Then you can get organized and start your new home with a clean slate.

5-Minutes or 5-Things

In five minutes, you can:

- Pack a small to mid-size box

- Take down the wall hangings from one room

- Make packing labels

- Fill out a change of address form

- Cancel or re-direct magazine subscriptions

Five things to put in a garage sale:

- Unwanted furniture

- Sports equipment you no longer use

- Old appliances and kitchenware

- Books

- Toys and clothing that kids have outgrown

Finding Movers

- Call a variety of moving companies to compare prices. Read the contracts carefully, and check with the Better Business Bureau before you sign a contract. Ask about whether rates are different for weekday and weekend or if they charge overtime.

- Get references and recommendations from friends.

- If you are packing your own items, be sure you get instructions from the moving company on how to do it so the items make it through the move without getting broken. Many companies offer brochures.

- If you are having the moving company do the job, pack the items you value the most, including antiques and jewelry, and personally transport these to your new home.

- Ensure that you have the name and phone number of the moving company or its representative at the point of origin and destination. Get the driver's name and phone number.

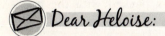 **Dear Heloise:**

Moving is a great incentive to go through the house, pick out those things you no longer need, and have a yard sale. The proceeds will help defray the cost of hiring a moving company.

Packing Up

- Sort and pack each room separately, keeping kitchen items away from bathroom items, etc. This will make unpacking much easier.

- Wrap dishes and breakable items in clean towels, washcloths, sheets, pillowcases, or even clothing.

- Use suitcases, duffel bags, trunks, and totes to hold your clothes. When packing clothes, pack only enough to fit without wrinkling. If you stuff them in, you'll have a lot of ironing to do when you unpack. Let your children pack their clothes in their own luggage.

- Pack books on edge in cartons. Use several smaller boxes for books rather than large ones. They'll be easier to lift.

- If your refrigerator or freezer will be moved and closed up, place charcoal or unused dry coffee grounds or baking soda into a cloth bag or old sock and toss inside. When you unpack and open it, there won't be a musty odor.

■ When you take down wall hangings or pictures, take the nails or hooks from the wall and tape them to the back of each item. After the move, you won't be looking for the right-size nail or hook.

■ Put together a "first night" box packed with the basics you'll need for your first night in your new home or apartment. Take this with you in your car, because moving vans can be delayed, as many of us have learned.

■ Toss a variety of plastic drop cloths in your car to take to your new home. Put them over the carpets to prevent dirt from being dragged in during the move. Old flannel-backed plastic tablecloths can protect varnished or new flooring from scratches.

■ Personally pack important documents such as wills, financial and property records, and valuables such as jewelry and old photographs. Take them with you in the car or plane, or store them in a safe-deposit box during the move.

■ If you move frequently, save the carton and packing when you buy bulky items, such as a lamp or a computer. Store the boxes flat and put packing materials in plastic bags. You won't have to buy these hard-to-find containers for the next move.

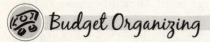 *Budget Organizing*

- Save plastic and paper bags, newspapers, and bubble wrap. They can be used to wrap and secure all kinds of breakable items.

- Save foam trays and egg cartons to place between fragile items like dishware.

- Ask for cardboard boxes from supermarkets or home improvement stores. You will need all you can get. It will save you a lot of money, too, if you don't have to buy them.

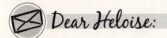 *Dear Heloise:*

The boxes that copy machine paper comes in are great help when moving. They are sturdy and have tight-fitting lids. They can be found at printing departments of high schools or colleges, copy stores, or office-supply stores.

Labeling Boxes

- Put fluorescent file labels on each box with the intended room written on them. For boxes that are to be stored, write the contents on the side and the end of the box.

- Mark boxes clearly with the intended room and box number. Maintain an inventory list with the number and contents of each box.

- After you've labeled kids' boxes, let your children mark them with their favorite stickers.

- Remember that the first box put in a moving van will be the last to come out, so arrange boxes accordingly.

- When packing valuables, do not indicate on the outside of the container what's inside. Give the box a number, and keep a listing of the contents on a separate card or page that will remain in your possession. Most movers are hon-est, but some might not be.

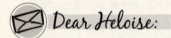 Dear Heloise:

When packing for a move, use a black marker to label boxes that contain items that are seldom used or will not be used for six months. Use a red marker to label boxes containing items that will need to be unpacked first. This way it should be easy to decide which boxes go to storage.

Create a Moving Countdown

The minute you learn you are moving, create a time line—a countdown to your official moving day. Breaking up this enor-mous job into smaller tasks makes moving more orderly and less overwhelming. Refer to your list and check off accomplished tasks. Here is a sample list of tasks:

Seven to Eight Weeks Before

- Get a large notebook to write in or to keep information and all receipts or anything pertaining to your move. Put it in a basket or bin so you know where all the data is.

- Write a list of all people who must be notified about your move: your family and friends, credit card companies, the bank, your children's schools, and your doctors and dentists.

■ Go to the post office for a change of address kit.

■ Call a variety of moving companies to compare prices and get references.

■ Check with your insurance agent to see if your home-owner's or renter's insurance policy covers your belongings in transit. Or obtain insurance in an amount sufficient to cover your possessions. Find out what the mover's insurance covers.

■ If your house is not yet on the market, find a good local real estate agent to prepare it for selling.

■ Assess everything in your house. Make a list of what goes with you and will be in your moving sale or what will be going to charity. Start making those A-B-C piles.

■ Take a trip to your new city to check out schools and the services of the community. Make a list! If you are not sure of the exact location, use the Internet sites for those cities and go to the local newspaper websites for more information.

■ If you are not driving to your new home, make flight and car rental reservations.

Five to Six Weeks Before

■ Decide on the moving company and clarify all the details of the move, such as the amount of packing you will do, and all the costs, including whether you need to have a cashier's or certified check on moving day.

■ Get a written appraisal on the value of any pricey antiques or objects you are moving.

■ Fill out and send all those change of address cards. Don't forget to change all your magazine subscription addresses to your new one.

■ Get copies of all your family records from your dentist, doctors, and veterinarian.

■ If you will be moving into an apartment building, make reservations for elevator use.

A Month Before

■ Start accumulating boxes, newspapers, bubble wrap, labels, and markers.

■ Use those boxes! Pack items you won't be using in the next few weeks.

■ If your move is to a distant location, make hotel reservations and get maps.

Three Weeks Before

■ Sort out the garage, attic, and other storage areas. Pack those items you will take; toss out the rest. Check with the moving company about transporting household chemicals; they may not take items such as flammables or chemicals, paint, or ammunition. Propane tanks must be emptied and sealed by a professional.

- Check with the post office to make sure your address-change notification is on record.

- Figure what you are going to do with your plants. You may have to give them away or carry them in your car. They can't be put inside a hot moving truck.

- Make plans for caring for your children and pets on moving day. Book your neighbor or a baby-sitter.

Two Weeks Before

- Set up the date that your utilities and phone service will be shut off or transferred in a local move. Just take note that your movers will need electricity, so the power should be shut off the day after the move.

- Retain your phone service during the move or use your cell phone. Keep your cell phone service because you will need it while you are traveling to your new home.

- Establish the date the utilities and phone service should be turned on in your new home.

- Get your car tuned up and in good road condition for a long-distance drive.

- Eat all the foods in your freezer or give them away.

- Continue packing items on a room-by-room basis.

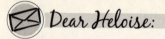 *Dear Heloise:*

When moving, we made a chart showing where all the pieces of crystal and china were placed in our buffet and one for the items in the curio. We used the charts when unpacking and put everything in its original place without all the fuss of wondering where the pieces would go.

One Week Before

- ▪ Reconfirm date and all arrangements with the moving company.

- ▪ Do banking: Get a cashier's or certified check for the movers, traveler's checks for your move, and close out your accounts.

- ▪ Refill any prescriptions you may need during your move.

- ▪ Defrost the freezer and clean the refrigerator.

- ▪ Drain out all oil and gas from lawn mowers, snow blowers, and snowmobiles.

- ▪ Check to make sure you have returned all library books and movie rentals.

- ▪ Cancel newspaper subscriptions.

- ▪ Continue packing. Keep a numbered list of all boxes.

Moving Day

- Supervise the movers, and if they are packing, watch the process and keep your list of all the boxes.

- When the van is packed, make a final inspection of your home.

- Double-check the bill of lading closely.

- Check phone numbers to ensure that you can be reached and so can the movers.

- Pack all the last-minute items.

- Shut down your home, turn off thermostats, and double-check to see that everything is turned off. Lock the doors and windows.

- Before the moving truck leaves, check each room and closet one last time. Check the attic and garage. Check the storage shed.

- If your home is still on the market, make certain the real estate agent has the keys.

- The police in your neighborhood should be informed that the house is vacant.

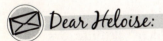 Dear Heloise:

For moving day, arrange away-from-the-house care for babies and small children. Have kids stay with a neighbor, friend, or family member nearby until you're ready to leave. You need all your attention on supervising and managing the move.

Move-In Day at Your New Home

- Make certain you arrive before the movers.

- Have utilities and the phone turned on and operating.

- Tell the movers exactly where you want the furniture and the boxes put.

- Look at everything carefully to see if it has been damaged.

- Count all the boxes. Compare the bill of lading with your personal checklist before signing and turning over the cashier's or certified check.

Heloise's "First Night" Box

Change of clothes for each
family member
Bedding
Towels
Toilet paper
Bar soap
Shower curtain and hooks
Lightbulbs
Flashlights
Breakfast items (bowls,
spoons, and cereal)

Dishwashing soap
Paper plates
Medications
Toothbrushes
Toothpaste
Paper cups
Pet food and dishes
Children's favorite toys
or games

Dear Heloise:

Set up your bed first. Then you can stop and rest when you need to. You can always go out for fast food when you're hungry, but it is no fun trying to set up your bed when you're already exhausted.

Dear Reader: All military families know this hint. We moved so many times, this was the number one hint I learned!

E-mail: Heloise @Heloise.com
Website: www.Heloise.com
Fax: 210-Heloise (435-6473)
Mail: PO Box 795000, San Antonio, TX 78279

Index

Page numbers in **bold** indicate tables.

A-B-C method for
  closets, 41
  garage, 62
  kitchen, 17, 20
  living room, 34
  moving, 163
  organizing basic, 5–7
  purse organization, 134
Activated charcoal for musty smells, 67
Add-on fare, 141
Addresses, 97
Advance planning for
  entertaining, 107, 108
  travel and vacations, 139–40
Airtight sealing, 24–25
Air travel, 140–41, 152–53
Aisles, shopping list organized by, 127, 132
All-inclusive price, 141
Answering machines and travel, 156
Appliance safety, 118
Appointments, 97
Armoires for home office, 93
Attic and basement, 66–69
  activated charcoal for, 67
  cleaning, 67
  container recycling for, 68
  5-Minutes/5-Things, 69
  flashlight for, 67
  holiday decorations, 68
  inventory for, 66–67, 68–69
  labeling for, 66, 68–69
  musty smells, 67, 68
  popcorn tins for, 68
  safety, 67
  seasonal organization for, 66, 67
  "zones" for, 66, 69
Automatic garage-door openers, 155

Baby-proofing kitchen, 28
Backpack for travel, 146
Bags for laundry, 58–59
Bandage boxes (metal), 74
Barbecue safety, 117
Basement. *See* Attic and basement
Baskets, 26
Bathrooms, 50–55
  budget organizing, 52–53
  caddies for, 52
  cleaners, 51
  cleaning after use, 50
  container recycling for, 52–53
  cosmetics, 52, 53
  cover-up containers for, 52
  drawers, 52
  family assignments, 50–51
  fishing-tackle box for, 53
  5-Minutes/5-Things, 51

Bathrooms (*cont.*)
  floor storage, avoiding, 50
  hair accessories, 52
  hanging baskets for, 52
  labeling for, 54
  medicine chest, 54–55
  potato chip cans for, 52
  revolving trays for, 52
  right stuff in right place, 50
  rules for, 50
  safety, 54, 55
  shelves over toilet for, 52
  shoe bags for, 52
  shower shelves for, 52
  squeegee for, 52
  tissue boxes for, 53
  turntable for, 53
  usage and item location, 54
Bathtub (infant), 77
Bed, setting up after moving, 169
Bed linens, 45–46
Bedrooms, 37–40
  budget organizing, 40
  classic hint, 40
  container recycling for, 40
  doors (back of) for, 39
  drawers, 39, 40
  exercise equipment, 39
  5-Minutes/5-Things, 38
  hooks for, 39, 40
  jewelry, 39–40
  labeling for, 40
  nightgown, 40
  nightlights, 39
  pajamas, 40
  paths, keeping clear, 39
  pocket contents, 39
  shoes, 40
  socks, 40
  under-bed storage, 39, 46
  underwear, 40
  See also Closets
Beverages, 113–15, **115**
Big-party planning, 118–20
Bill paying, 102–6
  calendar for, 103
  checkbook register, maintaining, 104
  companies, information about, 105
  credit cards, 105, 134–35, 143
  due dates for, 103
  late charges, 103
  lost credit cards, 105
  mailing bills, 103

  notebook for, 103
  paper, handling once, 91
  passports, 105
  personal files, throwing out, 106
  photocopying credit cards, 105
  self-employed bookkeeping system, 106
  stolen credit cards, 105
  tax filing, 105–6
  tracking hints, 103
  See also Personal organizing
Binders for schedules, 79
Blankets, 46
Bleach caution, 59
Boarding pets, 88–89
Bookcases, 42, 94
Books
  living room, 35–36
  packing, 159
Boxes for moving, 161
Breadbox, 19–20
Breakable items, packing, 159, 160–61
Breakfasts and children, 78, 81
Bubble wrap, 160
Budget organizing for
  bathrooms, 52–53
  bedrooms, 40
  closets, 44
  entertaining, 114
  grocery shopping, 132–33
  home office, 94, 95
  kid's stuff, 77
  kitchen, 16, 18, 23
  living room, 31, 32, 36
  moving, 160–61
  pets, 84
Bulk, buying items in, 136
Bulk foods, 24
Bulky items, kitchen, 15
Business cards, 98

Cabinets, kitchen, 17–21
Caddies for bathrooms, 52
Calendars for
  bill paying, 103
  children's schedules, 78, 80
  home office, 95
  personal organizing, 99
  pets, 83, 84
  travel, 152
Candle safety, 117
Canned Food Information Council, 21
Canned foods, 21
Cans (garbage) with wheels, 64

Caps from fabric softener or liquid detergent, 60
Cards, 99
Care instructions for clothes, 59
Carriers for pets, 88
Carry-on bag, 145, 147–48, **148**
Cars
  leaving pets inside, 88
  protection in garage, 65
  travel, 146, **149**, 149–52
Cat beds, 87
Caterers, 118, 119
CDs, 37
Centerpieces, 116
Chain for closets, 42
Champagne, 114
Charities and organizing, 2, 6–7
Checkbook cover for coupons, 132
Checkbook register, maintaining, 104
Children
  moving and, 167–68
  travel and, 148, 149–50
  See also Kid's stuff
Christmas cards, 100
Classic hint, 47
Cleaners
  in bathrooms, 51
  in kitchen, 18, 20, 21, 28
Cleaning after use, bathrooms, 50
Cleaning as you go, kitchen, 14
Closet for home office, 93
Closets, 41–49
  A-B-C method, 41
  bed linens, 45–46
  blankets, 46
  bookcases for, 42
  budget organizing, 44
  chain for, 42
  classic hints, 45, 47
  coat closets, 47–49
  color-coding for, 41, 49
  curtain rod for, 46
  dirty clothes, 43
  doors (back of) for, 39, 42
  furs, 43
  garbage cans (plastic) for, 44
  gloves, 48
  handbags, 42
  hangers for, 41–42
  hats, 48
  heirloom clothing, 43
  hooks for, 42, 47, 48
  inventory for, 49

keys, 47, 48–49
kids and, 77
  labeling for, 42, 44, 77
  laundry hamper for, 46
  leather clothes, 43
  linen closets, 45–47
  matching clothes, one hanger, 42
  milk crates for, 42
  outdoor gear, 47
  photo identification for, 42
  pillows, 46
  purses, 44, 133–35
  rearranging closets, 42–43
  seasonal clothing, 44, 48
  shelves for, 42
  shoes, 42, 43
  short items, 42
  storing clothes, 43–44
  suitcases for, 42
  sunlight damage, 43
  sweaters, 42
  tablecloths, 46
  under-the-shelf storage, 47
  usage and item location, 47
  work-week wardrobe planning, 44–45, 81
Clothing, children's, 76–77
Clutter bug quiz, 4
Clutter wars, 1
Coat closets, 47–49
Coffee cans, 65, 74
Cold weather and pets, 85–86
Collar for pets, 88
Color-coding for
  closets, 41, 49
  kid's stuff, 76, 78, 80
  kitchen, 21, 22, 27
  laundry, 57, 60
  living room, 35–36, 37
  moving, 162
Computers, 95
Container recycling for
  attic and basement, 68
  bathrooms, 52–53
  bedrooms, 40
  entertaining, 114, 120
  garage, 64–65
  home office, 94
  kid's stuff, 74–75
  kitchen, 18
  laundry, 60
  moving, 160
  pets, 84, 86

Cords, 28, 95, 118
Corks for finger protection, 16
Cosmetics, 52, 53
Countdown (timeline) for moving, 162–68
Counter for sorting laundry, 55
Coupons, 125–26, 127, 132–33
Cover-up containers for bathrooms, 52
Credit cards, 105, 134–35, 143
Culling (throwing things out), 2, 5–6
Curtain rod for closets, 46

Daily schedule for pets, 83
Dangerous items in garage, 63
Data on computer, cleaning up, 95
Dating foods, 21, 25, 27
Day care planning, 81
Deck/patio supplies, 63
Decorating information notebook, 31
Decorations, 115–16
Desk, 94
Detergent, 59
Diet for pets, 83–84, 89
Dirty clothes, 43
Disks, 96
Disposal of personal documents, 91–92
Documents
    packing important documents, 160
    travel and, 142–43, **143–44**
"Do not disturb" sign, 93
Doors (back of), 39, 42
Double-duty shelf, 36
Drawers
    bathrooms, 52
    bedrooms, 39, 40
    kitchen, 17–21
Drop cloths for floor protection, 160
Due dates for bill paying, 103
Duffel bags, 58
Dusting ease, 30
DVDs, 37

Eating before grocery shopping, 135
Egg cartons, 40
Electronic calendars, 95
Electronic locators, 9
Emergencies
    entertaining and, 117–18
    pets and, 83, 85, 88
Emergency checklist for personal organizing, 100–101

Emergency organizing kit, 8, **8**
Entertaining, 107–21
    advance planning for, 107, 108
    appliance safety, 118
    barbecue safety, 117
    beverages, 113–15, **115**
    big-party planning, 118–20
    budget organizing, 114
    candle safety, 117
    caterers, 118, 119
    centerpiece, 116
    champagne, 114
    classic hint, 109
    container recycling for, 114, 120
    cord safety, 118
    decorations, 115–16
    emergencies, 117–18
    files for, 120–21
    guidelines for, 107–8
    help, accepting, 108
    ice cubes, 114
    invitations, 110–11, 118
    jigger for measuring drinks, 113
    keepsake of memorable party, 116
    leftovers from, 121
    liquor, 113–15, **115**
    list-making for, 107, 109–11
    map in invitations, 111
    menu planning, **111–12**, 111–13
    outdoor parties, 118
    place cards, 116
    safety, 117–18
    serving ideas, 115–16
    servingware, 115, 116–17
    shopping list for, **111–12**
    simplicity for, 108
    small parties vs. large party, 109
    S-M-I-L-E for, 109
    what (kind) of party, 110
    when (date and time) of party, 110
    where (location) of party, 110
    who (guest list) for, 110
    wine, 113–14
Envelopes for coupons, 132, 133
Exercise equipment, 39
Exercise for pets, 85–86

Family assignments for bathrooms, 50–51
Family organization. *See* Entertaining; Kid's stuff; Organizing basics; Personal organizing; Pets
Fax cover sheet, 95

Feeding
  pets, 83–84, 89
  sick child, 80
Files for
  entertaining, 120–21
  personal organization, 93, 94, 98
Filing cabinets, 93
Film canisters for small items, 94
Financial records, 101–2
Fines for mess in garage, 66
"First night" box, 160, **168**
Fishing-tackle box, 53, 61
5-Minutes/5-Things
  attic and basement, 69
  bathrooms, 51
  bedrooms, 38
  garage, 69
  kitchen, 14
  laundry, 56
  living room, 30–31
  moving, 157–58
  organizing basic, 3, 5
  personal organizing, 92
Flashlights, 67
Floor storage, avoiding, 50
Fly-drive tour, 141
Focal point, creating, 31–32
Folding clothes, 60
Food, putting away, 14
Food storage for pets, 86
Footlockers, 77
Force majeure, 141
Freezer, 24–27, 25–26, 159
Frozen items, cooler for, 136
"Fun box" for sick child, 80
Fun storage solutions, 74–75
Furniture for office, 93–94
Furs, 43

Games and toys, 36
Garage, 62–66
  A-B-C method, 62
  cans with wheels, 64
  car protection, 65
  container recycling for, 64–65
  dangerous items, 63
  fines for mess, 66
  5-Minutes/5-Things, 69
  gardening tools, 65
  glass (see-through) containers, 64
  grill accessories, 63
  hammock for, 63
  hangers for, 65
  hanging racks for, 62, 63
  hooks for, 65
  hoses, 65
  joists for, 64
  labeling for, 63
  like items together for, 63
  outlined areas for, 65–66, 69
  padding for, 65
  parking guides, 65
  patio/deck supplies, 63
  Peg-Board for, 64
  photo identification for, 64
  reflector tape for, 65
  right stuff in right place, 62
  rolling carts for, 63
  seasonal organization of items, 62–63
  shelves for, 62
  sports equipment, 63
  tools, 64–65
  utility racks for, 62, 63
Garage/yard sale before moving, 157, 159
Garbage bags, 16
Garbage cans (plastic), 44, 86
Gardening tools, 65
Glass (see-through) containers, 16, 22, 24, 64
Gloves, 48
Greeting cards, 99
Grill accessories, 63
Grocery shopping, 125–36
  aisles, list organized by, 127, 132
  budget organizing, 132–33
  bulk, buying items in, 136
  checkbook cover for coupons, 132
  coupons, 125–26, 127, 132–33
  eating before, 135
  envelopes for coupons, 132, 133
  frozen items, cooler for, 136
  impulse shopping, avoiding, 126, 135
  labels of foods for list, 131–32
  lists, 125, 126–32, **128–31**, 135
  menus, making in advance, 125, 126
  precooked/packing, avoiding, 136
  preprinted grocery list, 127, **128–31**
  purse organizing for, 133–35
  recipes, saving, 127
  shopping for others, 131–32
  strategies, 125–26
  supermarket specials for, 126
  timing for, 135
  weekly trips, 126, 127
  See also Kitchen; Shopping

Groups of toys, 76
Guarantees, 17

Hair accessories, 52
Hammocks, 63, 75
Hampers for clothes, 57
Handbags, 42
Hangers, 41–42, 65
Hanging baskets, 18, 52
Hanging clothes after drying, 59
Hanging pictures, 33, 160
Hanging racks, 62, 63, 75
Harness for pets, 88
Hats, 48
Health care for pets, 84–85
Heirloom clothing, 43
Heloise contact information, 170
Helping others and organizing, 2,
    6–7
Help with entertaining, accepting,
    108
Hidden spaces for living room, 30
Holiday decorations, 68
Holidays. See Entertaining
Home electronics, 36–37
Home office, 92–96
    armoires for, 93
    bookcase, 94
    budget organizing, 94, 95
    calendars, 95
    closet for, 93
    computers, 95
    container recycling for, 94
    cord organizers, 95
    data on computer, cleaning up, 95
    desk, 94
    disks, 96
    "do not disturb" sign for, 93
    electronic calendars, 95
    fax cover sheet, 95
    file storage, 94
    filing cabinet for, 93
    film canisters for small items, 94
    furniture for, 93–94
    in/out baskets, 94
    magazine articles, saving, 96, 98
    milk crates for, 94
    newspaper articles, saving, 96, 98
    pencil holders, 94
    rolling desk system for, 93
    space for, 93
    See also Personal organizing
Home safety during travel, 155–56

Hooks for
    bedrooms, 39, 40
    closets, 42, 47, 48
    garage, 65
    kitchen, 23
Hoses, 65
Hotels, 153–55
Hot weather and pets, 85, 88
House organization. See Attic and
    basement; Bathrooms; Bedrooms;
    Closets; Garage; Kitchen; Laundry
    room; Living room; Organizing
    basics
House-sitting services, 156

Ice-cream cartons, 75
Ice cubes, 114
Ice cube trays, 40
Identification
    luggage, 145–46, 153
    pets, ID tags, 88
Identity theft, 92
Impulse shopping, avoiding, 126, 135
In/out baskets, 94
Inspection of luggage, 153
Instruction booklets, 17
Instructions for laundry, 55, 56, 58
Insurance for travel, 141–42, 152
Inventory for
    attic and basement, 66–67, 68–69
    closets, 49
    kitchen, 26, 27
Invitations, 110–11, 118
Ironing, avoiding, 59
Irreplaceable documents, 102

Jewelry, 39–40
Jigger for measuring drinks, 113
Joists, 64
Juice cans, 75
"Junk" drawer, 16, 18
Junk mail, 91

Keepsake of memorable party, 116
Kennels, researching, 88–89
Keys, 47, 48–49
Kid's stuff, 73–81
    bandage boxes (metal) for, 74
    bathtub (infant) for, 77
    binders for schedules, 79
    breakfasts and, 78, 81
    budget organizing, 77
    calendar for schedules, 78, 80

clothing, 76–77
coffee cans for, 74
color-coding for, 76, 78, 80
container recycling for, 74–75
day care planning, 81
feeding sick child, 80
footlocker for, 77
"fun box" for sick child, 80
fun storage solutions, 74–75
groups of toys, 76
hammock for, 75
hanging racks for, 75
ice-cream cartons for, 75
juice cans for, 75
labeling for, 76, 77
laundry baskets for, 75
lunch packing, 78
matching clothes, one hanger/bag, 76
milk jugs for, 74
mornings and, 78, 81
muffin tin for feeding sick child, 80
papers that need signing, 78
personalized toy box for, 75
putting away laundry, 77
puzzles, 75
revolving trays for, 80
right stuff in right place, 73
schedules and, 78
school papers, 79
sick children and, 80–81
sizes of clothing, labeling, 77
storage aids, 74
thermos for sick child, 81
toys, 36, 75–76
trash cans for, 75
under-bed storage, 75
wading pool for, 75
wardrobe (weekly) planning, 81
See also Children
Kitchen, 13–28
A-B-C method, 17, 20
airtight sealing for, 24–25
baby-proofing kitchen, 28
baskets for, 26
breadbox, 19–20
budget organizing, 16, 18, 23
bulk foods, 24
bulky items, 15
cabinets, 17–21
canned foods, 21
classic hints, 20, 22
cleaners, 18, 20, 21, 28
cleaning as you go, 14

color-coding for, 21, 22, 27
container recycling for, 18
cords, 28
corks for finger protection, 16
dating foods, 21, 25, 27
drawers, 17–21
5-Minutes/5-Things, 14
food, putting away, 14
freezer, 25–26
garbage bags, 16
general hints, 15–16
glass (see-through) containers, 16, 22, 24
guarantees, 17
hanging baskets for, 18
hooks for, 23
instruction booklets, 17
inventory for, 26, 27
"junk" drawer, 16, 18
knives, 16, 28
labeling for, 25, 26
leftovers, 24, 25
lights (push lights) in cabinets, 18
lining cabinet shelves, 18–19
packaged foods, 18, 136
pantry, 21–23
paper plates, uses for, 15
paper towel cardboard cores for, 23
photo identification for, 19
pots and pans, 18
putting away food, 14
refrigerator and freezer, 24–27, 159
rules for, 13–14
safety, 27–28
shelf liners, 18–19
shelves, 18, 19
soups and stews, 25
spices, 15, 18
turntable for, 18
under-the-cabinet storage, 19
under-the-shelf storage, 23
under-the-sink storage, 20
usage and item location, 15, 20, 23, 24, 25
utensils, 15–16, 18, 28
See also Grocery shopping
Knives, 16, 28

Labeling for
attic and basement, 66, 68–69
bathrooms, 54
bedrooms, 40
closets, 42, 44, 77

Labeling for (*cont.*)
  garage, 63
  kid's stuff, 76, 77
  kitchen, 25, 26
  living room, 35, 37
  moving, 161–62
  personal organizing, 97–98
  pets, 87
  suitcase, 145
Labels of foods for grocery list,
  131–32
Ladders, 32
Late charges, 103
Laundry baskets, 75
Laundry hampers, 46
Laundry list, 57
Laundry room, 55–61
  bags for, 58–59
  bleach caution, 59
  care instructions, 59
  classic hint, 58–59
  color-coding for, 57, 60
  container recycling for, 60
  counter for, 55
  detergent, 59
  duffel bags for, 58
  fishing-tackle box for, 61
  5-Minutes/5-Things, 56
  folding clothes, 60
  hampers for, 57
  hanging clothes after drying, 59
  instructions for laundry, 55, 56, 58
  ironing, avoiding, 59
  laundry list, **57**
  lint-collectors/producers, 58
  overloading caution, 59
  pincushions, 61
  putting away laundry, 60, 77
  sewing kit for, 56, 61
  shelves for, 55
  socks, 58
  sorting, 57–59
  stains, 59
  thread spools, 61
  underwear sets, 60
  washing and drying, 56, 59
  water temperature, 59
Leashes for pets, 86
Leather clothes, 43
Ledge for shelf, 36
Leftovers
  entertaining, 121
  food, 24, 25

Lights (push lights) in cabinets, 18
Like items together, 63
Linen closets, 45–47
Lining cabinet shelves, 18–19
Lint-collectors/producers, 58
Liquor, 113–15, **115**
List-making for
  entertaining, 107, 109–11
  grocery shopping, 125, 126–32,
    128–31, 135
  guest list, 110
  labels of foods for list, 131–32
  laundry, 57
  menu planning, **111–12**
  organizing basic, 7–8
  personal organizing, 100–101
  to-do lists, 7–8, 98
Living room, 29–37
  A-B-C method, 34
  books, 35–36
  budget organizing, 31, 32, 36
  CDs, 37
  color-coding for, 35–36, 37
  decorating information notebook, 31
  double-duty shelf, 36
  dusting ease and, 30
  DVDs, 37
  5-Minutes/5-Things, 30–31
  focal point, creating, 31–32
  games and toys, 36
  hanging pictures, 33, 160
  hidden spaces for, 30
  home electronics, 36–37
  labeling for, 35, 37
  ladders for, 32
  ledge for shelf, 36
  magazines, 30, 36
  newspapers, 30
  photos, 31–32, 33, 34–35
  picture hanging, 33, 160
  popcorn tins for, 36
  remote controls, 36
  right stuff in right place, 29
  rules for, 29
  sewing projects, 36
  videotapes, 37
  wall hangings, 32–33, 160
  window seat for, 30
Lost
  credit cards, 105
  luggage prevention, 153
  pets, 89–90
Lunch packing, 78

Magazine articles, saving, 96, 98
Magazines, 30, 36
Mail, holding during travel, 156
Mailing bills, 103
Map in invitations, 111
Margarine tubs, 18, 74, 84
Matching clothes, one hanger/bag, 42, 76
Medical requirements for travel, 140, 143
Medications for pets, 84
Medicine chest, 54–55
Memo books, 97–98
Menu planning for
    entertaining, **111–12,** 111–13
    grocery shopping, 125, 126
Milk crates, 42, 94
Milk jugs, 74
Mornings and children, 78, 81
Movers, finding, 158–59
Moving, 157–69
    A-B-C method, 163
    bed, setting up first, 169
    books, packing, 159
    boxes for, 161
    breakable items, packing, 159, 160–61
    budget organizing, 160–61
    children and, 167–68
    color-coding for, 162
    container recycling for, 160
    countdown (timeline) for, 162–68
    documents (important), packing, 160
    drop cloths for floor protection, 160
    "first night" box, 160, **168**
    5-Minutes/5-Things, 157–58
    garage/yard sale before, 157, 159
    labeling for, 161–62
    movers, finding, 158–59
    packing, 159–61
    pets and, 167–68
    pictures, keeping nails, 160
    refrigerator/freezer, packing, 159
    rooms, packing separately, 159
    unpacking, 166
    valuables, packing, 160, 161–62
    wall hangings, keeping nails, 160
Muffin tins, 40, 80
Mugs (cracked or chipped), 94
Music for chores, 5
Musty smells, 67, 68

Newspaper articles, saving, 96, 98
Newspapers, 30
Nightgown, 40
Nightlights, 39

Notebooks, 97–98, 103
Nursery flats, 94

Occasions, remembering, 98–100
Office. *See* Home office
On the go and organizing. *See* Grocery
    shopping; Moving; Organizing basics;
    Shopping; Travel and vacations
Organizers, personal, 96–101
Organizing basics, 1–10
    charities and, 2, 6–7
    clutter bug quiz, 4
    clutter wars, 1
    electronic locators, 9
    emergency organizing kit, 8, 8
    helping others and, 2, 6–7
    music for chores, 5
    problem areas, 10
    starting, keys for, 2–3
    storage aids, 8–9, **9,** 74
    throwing away (culling), 2, 5–6
    time saved from, ix–x
    to-do lists, 7–8, 98
    TV-Commercial Cleaning Method, 3, 5
    See also A-B-C method; Attic and
    basement; Bathrooms; Bedrooms;
    Bill paying; Closets; Entertaining;
    5-Minutes/5-Things; Garage; Grocery
    shopping; Home office; Kid's stuff;
    Kitchen; Laundry room; List-making;
    Living room; Moving; Personal
    organizing; Pets; Right stuff in right
    place; Shopping; Travel and
    vacations; Usage and item location
Outdoor gear, 47
Outdoor parties, 118
Outlined areas for garage, 65–66, 69
Overloading washer/dryer caution, 59
Overnight bag, 146, 155

Packaged foods, 18, 136
Packing
    moving and, 159–61
    suitcase, 144–48, **146–48**
Padding for garage, 65
Pajamas, 40
Pantry, 21–23
Paper, handling once, 91
Paper plates, 15
Papers that need signing, 78
Paper towel cardboard cores, 23
Parking guides, 65
Parties. *See* Entertaining

Passports, 105
Paths, keeping clear, 39
Patio/deck supplies, 63
Peg-Board for garage, 64
Pencil holders, 94
Personal files, throwing out, 106
Personalized toy box, 75
Personal organizing, 91–106
  addresses, 97
  appointments, 97
  business cards, 98
  calendar for, 99
  cards, 99
  Christmas cards, 100
  classic hint, 102
  disposal of personal documents, 91–92
  emergency checklist for, 100–101
  filing system, 98
  financial records, 101–2
  5-Minutes/5-Things, 92
  greeting cards, 99
  identity theft, 92
  irreplaceable documents, 102
  junk mail, 91
  labeling for, 97–98
  memo books for, 97–98
  notebooks for, 97–98
  occasions, remembering, 98–100
  organizers, 96–101
  paper, handling once, 91
  photos for thank you notes, 99–100
  postcards, 99
  proof of ownership, 101
  remembering occasions, 98–100
  safe-deposit box for, 102
  shredders for, 91–92
  spelling-test notebooks for, 98
  thank you notes, 99–100
  to-do lists, 7–8, 98
  See also Bill paying; Home office
Pets, 82–90
  boarding pets, 88–89
  budget organizing, 84
  calendar for, 83, 84
  carriers, 88
  cars, leaving pets inside, 88
  cat beds, 87
  cold weather, 85–86
  collar, 88
  container recycling for, 84, 86
  daily schedule for, 83
  diet, 83–84, 89
  emergencies, 83, 85, 88
  exercise, 85–86
  feeding, 83–84, 89
  food storage, 86
  garbage can for food, 86
  harness, 88
  health care, 84–85
  hot weather and, 85, 88
  identification tags for, 88
  kennels, researching, 88–89
  labeling for, 87
  leashes, 86
  lost pets, 89–90
  medications, 84
  moving and, 167–68
  pet-sitters, 89
  rabies tag, 86
  safety, 82–83
  scoops for dry pet food, 84
  supplies, storing, 86–87
  toys, 86, 87
  travel and vacations, 83, 87–90
  vaccination information, 84
Pet-sitters, 89
Photocopying credit cards, 105
Photo identification for
  closets, 42
  garage, 64
  kitchen, 19
Photos
  decorating with, 31–32, 33, 34–35
  thank you notes and, 99–100
Picture hanging, 33, 160
Pillows, 46
Pincushions, 61
Place cards, 116
Plastic bags vs. luggage, 150
Pocket contents, 39
Popcorn tins, 36, 68
Postcards, 99
Potato chip cans, 52
Pots and pans, 18
Pre-cooked/packing, avoiding, 136
Preprinted grocery list, 127, **128–31**
Problem areas, organizing, 10
Proof of ownership, 101
Purses, 44, 133–35
Push lights in cabinets, 18
Putting away food, 14
Putting away laundry, 60, 77
Puzzles, 75

Rabies tag, 86
Rearranging closets, 42–43

Recipes, saving, 127
Recycled containers. *See* Container
    recycling
Reflector tape for garage, 65
Refrigerator and freezer, 24–27, 159
Remembering occasions, 98–100
Remote controls, 36
Renting car or recreational vehicle (RV),
    151–52
Reservations, 140, 142, 154
Revolving trays, 52, 80
Right stuff in right place
    bathrooms, 50
    garage, 62
    kid's stuff, 73
    living room, 29
    organizing basic, 2–3, 6, 8–9, **8–9**
Road trips, 146, **149**, 149–52
Rolling carts, 63
Rolling desk system, 93
Rooms, packing separately, 159

Safe-deposit box, 102
Safety
    attic and basement, 67
    bathrooms, 54, 55
    entertaining, 117–18
    home safety during travel, 155–56
    kitchen, 27–28
    pets, 82–83
Sales, **136–38**
Schedules and children, 78
School papers, 79
Scoops for dry pet food, 84
Seasonal organization for
    attic and basement, 66, 67
    clothing, 44, 48
    garage, 62–63
See-through containers, 16, 22, 24, 64
Self-employed bookkeeping system,
    106
Serving ideas, 115–16
Servingware, 115, 116–17
Sewing kits, 56, 61
Sewing projects, 36
Shelf liners, 18–19
Shelves for
    bathrooms, 52
    closets, 42
    garage, 62
    kitchen, 18, 19
    laundry, 55
Shoe bags/boxes, 40, 52

Shoes
    closets, 40, 42, 43
    packing, 145
Shopping, 125–38
    A-B-C method for purse, 134
    for others, 131–32
    purse organizing for, 133–35
    sales, **136–38**
    usage and item location, 134
    See also Grocery shopping
Shopping list for entertaining, **111–12**
Short items in closets, 42
Shower shelves, 52
Shredders, 91–92
Sick children, 80–81
Simplicity for entertaining, 108
Sizes of clothing, labeling, 77
Small parties vs. large party, 109
S-M-I-L-E for entertaining, 109
Socks, 40, 58
Sorting laundry, 57–59
Soups and stews, 25
Space for home office, 93
Spelling-test notebooks, 98
Spices, 15, 18
Sports equipment, 63
Squeegee for shower, 52
Stains on laundry, 59
Starting organizing, keys for, 2–3
Stolen credit cards, 105
Storage aids, 8–9, 9, 74
Storing clothes, 43–44
Suitcase packing, 144–48, **146–48**
Suitcases for storage, 42
Sunlight damage, 43
Supermarket specials, 126. *See also*
    Grocery shopping
Sweaters, 42

Tablecloths, 46
Tackle (fishing) box, 53, 61
Take-out food containers, 86
Tax filing, 105–6
Thank you notes, 99–100
Thermos for sick child, 81
Thread spools, 61
Throwing things out (culling), 2, 5–6
Timeline (countdown) for moving,
    162–68
Timers for home safety, 155
Time saved from organizing, ix–x
Timing for grocery shopping, 135
Tissue boxes, 53

To-do lists, 7–8, 98
Toiletries, 145, 147, **147**
Tools, 64–65
Toys
  kid's stuff, 75–76
  living room and, 36
  pets', 86, 87
Tracking bills, 103
Trash cans, 75
Travel agents, 140
Travel and vacations, 139–56
  add-on fare, 141
  advance planning for, 139–40
  air travel, 140–41, 152–53
  all-inclusive price, 141
  answering machines and, 156
  automatic garage-door openers, 155
  backpack for, 146
  calendar for, 152
  carry-on bag, 145, 147–48, **148**
  car travel, 146, **149**, 149–52
  children and, 148, 149–50
  credit cards and, 143
  documents for, 142–43, **143–44**
  fly-drive tour, 141
  force majeure, 141
  home safety during, 155–56
  hotels, 153–55
  house-sitting services, 156
  identification, luggage, 145–46, 153
  inspection of luggage, 153
  insurance for, 141–42, 152
  labeling suitcase, 145
  lost luggage prevention, 153
  mail, holding during, 156
  medical requirements for, 140, 143
  overnight bag, 146, 155
  packing suitcase, 144–48, **146–48**
  pets and, 83, 87–90
  plastic bags vs. luggage, 150
  renting car or recreational vehicle (RV),
    151–52
  reservations, 140, 142, 154
  road trips, 146, **149**, 149–52
  safety of home during, 155–56
  shoes, packing, 145
  suitcase packing, 144–48, **146–48**
  timers for home safety, 155
  toiletries, 145, 147, **147**
  travel agents, 140
  traveler's checks for, 143
  trip cancellation insurance, 142
  underwear in shoe box for, 155
  wrinkled clothing, preventing, 145
Traveler's checks, 143
Trip cancellation insurance, 142
Trips. See Travel and vacations
Turntables, 18, 53
TV-Commercial Cleaning Method, 3, 5

Under-bed storage, 39, 46, 75
Under-the-cabinet storage, 19
Under-the-shelf storage, 23, 47
Under-the-sink storage, 20
Underwear, 40, 60, 155
Unpacking, 166
Usage and item location
  bathrooms, 54
  closets, 47
  kitchen, 15, 20, 23, 24, 25
  organizing basic, 2, 5–6
  shopping, 134
Utensils, 15–16, 18, 28
Utility racks, 62, 63

Vacations. See Travel and vacations
Vaccination information for pets, 84
Valuables, packing, 160, 161–62
Videotapes, 37

Wading pools, 75
Wall hangings, 32–33, 160
Wardrobe (weekly) planning, 44–45, 81
Washing and drying clothes, 56, 59
Water temperature for washing, 59
Weekly trips to grocery, 126, 127
Weekly wardrobe planning, 44–45, 81
What (kind) of party, 110
When (date and time) of party, 110
Where (location) of party, 110
Who (guest list) for party, 110
Window seats, 30
Wine, 113–14
Work-week wardrobe planning, 44–45,
  81
Wrinkled clothing, preventing, 145

Yogurt cups, 18, 84, 94

"Zones" for attic and basement, 66, 69